Michigan
TrailMaps.com

www.michigantrailmaps.com

Web Site ❖ Books ❖ Maps ❖ Information

Isle Royale

National Park

Foot Trails & Water Routes

Fourth Edition

Jim DuFresne

Published by
MichiganTrailMaps.com
P.O. Box 852
Clarkston, MI 48347
www.michigantrailmaps.com

First edition 1984, 2nd edition 1991, 3rd edition 2002, 4th edition 2011

Proudly Manufactured in Michigan of the United States of America

Project Manager: Jessica DuFresne
Editor: Margaret Van DerGracht
Art on page 35 by Stephen R. Whitney
Maps: MichiganTrailMaps.com
Cover photograph: *Backpackers on the Rock Harbor Trail*
Photos by the author unless otherwise credited.

Library of Congress Cataloging in Publication Data
DuFresne, Jim.
Isle Royale National Park: Foot Trails & Water Routes / Jim DuFresne. – 4th edition
p. cm.
Includes bibliographical references and index.
ISBN 978-0-9830150-0-0
1. Hiking--Michigan--Isle Royale National Park--Guide-books.
    2. Backpacking--Michigan--Isle Royale National Park--Guide-books.
    3. Canoes and canoeing--Michigan--Isle Royale National Park--Guide-books. 4. Trails--Michigan--Isle Royale National Park--Guide-books. 5. Isle Royale National Park (Mich.)--Guide-books.
    L Title.
GV199.42.M5121843 2010   2002004130
917.74 ' 9970443--dc20
ISBN 13: 978-0-9830150-0-0

Author Appreciation

I deeply appreciate all the National Park Service rangers and officials who assisted me in researching the fourth edition of this guidebook, a book that has been around for almost 30 years. I also need to thank all the backpackers, hikers, paddlers and visitors that I encountered on the trails and along the waterways who passed along tips, suggestions, encouragement and even a little spare gorp. But most of all I need to thank my daughter, Jessica, for moving MichiganTrailMaps.com from a traditional print publisher to its online identity and Margaret Van DerGracht, my editor. Van DerGracht is one of the finest editors I've ever had, and I've had a bunch of them. A former English teacher, she ended the project by saying it was time for me to stop writing guidebooks and to start working on my Great American Novel. It's coming, Meg, it's coming.

j.d.

To my father, Harris DuFresne (1921-2001),
Who put sand in my shoes,
a pack on my back, and led me into the woods.
There are lessons to be learned among the trees,
he said.
j.d.

Hikers drop their packs and take a break to enjoy the view of Lake Desor from the Greenstone Ridge Trail.

Contents

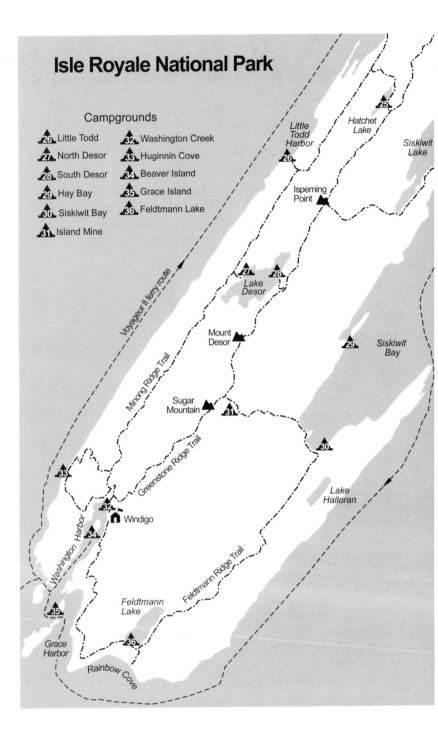

Isle Royale National Park

Campgrounds

- 26 Little Todd
- 27 North Desor
- 28 South Desor
- 29 Hay Bay
- 30 Siskiwit Bay
- 31 Island Mine
- 32 Washington Creek
- 33 Huginnin Cove
- 34 Beaver Island
- 35 Grace Island
- 36 Feldtmann Lake

Little Todd Harbor

Hatchet Lake

Siskiwit Lake

25

26

Ispeming Point

27

28

Lake Desor

Voyageur II ferry route

Minong Ridge Trail

Mount Desor

29

Siskiwit Bay

Sugar Mountain

31

30

Greenstone Ridge Trail

Lake Halloran

33

32

Windigo

34

Washington Harbor

35

Grace Harbor

Feldtmann Lake

Feldtmann Ridge Trail

36

Rainbow Cove

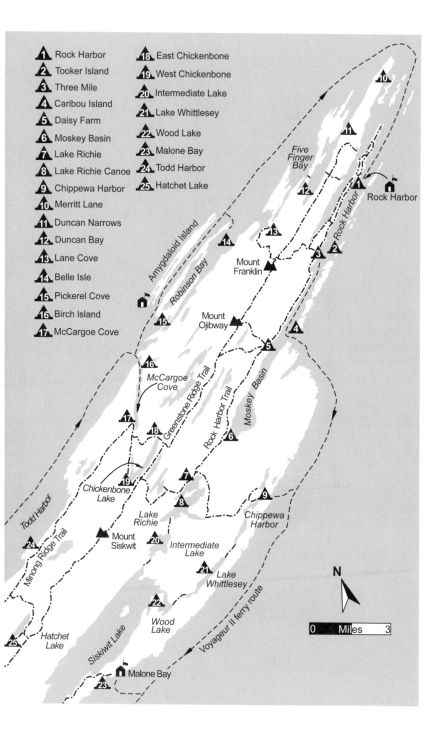

Foreword

The mystique of Isle Royale beckons through the mists and waters of Lake Superior. The journey to Isle Royale is a long one for most people. For some it may start with developing their skills to face the challenging trails or waters for boating For others, it may be just the combination of a long car, boat, or float plane ride to get to the island. The better prepared you are to hike or boat around the island the more enjoyment you will derive from this unique maritime environment.

This book is entering its 27th year of service and fourth edition of publishing. The fact that it has stood the test of time and readers' travels reflect the author's personal love of the island and commitment to keeping the guide current and relevant for readers.

Every visitor who comes to the island can make a difference for the future of the island....by helping keep the wildlife wild, by leaving no trace in your passage, by learning how to keep unwanted hitchhikers(exotic species) out of the park. In return the island will reward you with spectacular vistas, clear water, excellent fishing, and a chance to see and experience it's flora and fauna in a rare setting of wind, waves, and forests.

People share the park with the wildlife and each other. Mutual respect for all the creatures exploring this special place will enhance the experience for everyone. I hope this guidebook helps you plan and enjoy the trip ahead.

Phyllis Green
Superintendent, Isle Royale National Park

Trail Mileage Between Campgrounds

	Rock Harbor	Three Mile	Daisy Farm	Lane Cove	Moskey Basin	Lake Richie	East Chickenbone	West Chickenbone	Todd Harbor
Rock Harbor		2.7	7.1	6.9	11.0	12.9	13.3	14.8	22.2
Three Mile	2.7		4.4	4.6	8.3	10.2	10.5	12.5	19.5
Daisy Farm	7.1	4.4		6.9	3.9	5.8	6.1	7.9	14.9
Lane Cove	6.9	4.6	6.9		10.8	12.7	10.9	12.7	19.5
Moskey Basin	11.0	8.3	3.9	10.8		2.3	7.3	5.9	15.1
Lake Richie	12.9	10.2	5.8	12.7	2.3		5.0	3.6	13.0
East Chickenbone	13.3	10.5	6.1	10.9	7.3	5.0		1.8	8.7
West Chickenbone	14.8	12.5	7.9	12.7	5.9	3.6	1.8		9.3
Todd Harbor	22.2	19.5	14.9	19.5	15.1	13.0	8.7	9.3	
Chippewa Harbor	16.8	14.1	9.7	16.6	6.2	4.3	9.3	7.9	17.3
McCargoe Cove	15.3	12.6	8.2	13.0	8.4	6.3	2.1	2.7	6.7
Hatchet Lake	22.3	19.8	15.4	20.2	13.4	11.1	9.3	7.9	4.1
Malone Bay	34.3	31.6	27.2	30.5	23.7	23.0	19.6	18.2	15.0
Little Todd Harbor	28.6	25.9	21.5	26.5	22.1	18.5	15.6	16.2	7.0
North Desor	33.1	30.4	26.0	30.8	25.3	23.0	19.6	19.8	11.4
South Desor	29.4	26.7	22.5	27.3	20.5	18.2	16.4	15.0	11.8
Huginnin Cove	44.4	41.7	37.3	41.2	34.6	32.3	30.3	29.1	24.8
Washington Creek	40.1	37.8	33.2	38.3	31.0	28.9	27.1	25.7	23.0
Island Mine	34.3	31.6	27.4	32.2	25.4	23.1	21.3	19.9	16.7
Feldtmann Lake	49.0	46.3	41.9	46.7	40.1	37.0	35.8	34.4	31.8
Siskiwit Bay	38.7	36.0	31.8	36.6	29.8	27.5	25.7	24.3	21.1

Chippewa Harbor	McCargoe Cove	Hatchet Lake	Malone Bay	Little Todd Harbor	North Desor	South Desor	Huginnin Cove	Washington Creek	Island Mine	Feldtmann Lake	Siskiwit Bay
16.8	15.3	22.3	34.3	28.6	33.1	29.4	44.4	40.1	34.3	49.0	38.7
14.1	12.6	19.8	31.6	25.9	30.4	26.7	41.7	37.8	31.6	46.3	36.0
9.7	8.2	15.4	27.2	21.5	26.0	22.5	37.3	33.2	27.4	41.9	31.8
16.6	13.0	20.2	30.5	26.5	30.8	27.3	41.2	38.3	32.2	46.7	36.6
6.2	8.4	13.4	23.7	22.1	25.3	20.5	34.6	31.0	25.4	40.1	29.8
4.3	6.3	11.1	21.4	18.5	23.0	18.2	32.3	28.9	23.1	37.8	27.5
9.3	2.1	9.3	19.6	15.6	19.6	16.4	30.3	27.1	21.3	35.8	25.7
7.9	2.7	7.9	18.2	16.2	19.8	15.0	29.1	25.7	19.9	34.4	24.3
17.3	6.7	4.1	15.0	7.0	11.4	11.8	24.8	23.0	16.7	31.8	21.1
■	10.6	15.2	25.7	22.6	27.3	22.5	36.4	33.0	27.2	42.0	31.6
10.6	■	10.7	20.9	13.5	18.0	17.7	31.8	28.4	22.6	37.1	27.0
15.2	10.7	■	11.3	7.8	12.3	8.1	25.7	18.8	13.0	27.6	17.4
25.7	20.9	11.3	■	18.7	23.2	10.8	24.9	21.5	15.7	30.3	20.1
22.6	13.5	7.8	18.7	■	5.7	15.5	19.1	17.3	20.4	26.1	24.8
27.3	18.0	12.3	23.2	5.7	■	20.0	14.4	12.0	18.6	21.4	23.0
22.5	17.7	8.1	10.8	14.9	20.0	■	14.7	11.3	5.5	20.1	9.9
36.4	31.8	25.7	24.9	19.1	14.4	14.7	■	4.0	10.0	12.8	14.4
33.0	28.4	18.8	21.5	17.3	12.0	11.3	4.0	■	6.6	8.8	11.0
27.2	22.6	13.0	15.7	20.4	18.6	5.5	10.0	6.6	■	14.6	4.4
42.0	37.1	27.6	30.3	26.1	21.4	20.1	12.8	8.8	14.6	■	10.3
31.6	27.0	17.4	20.1	24.8	23.0	9.9	14.4	11.0	4.4	10.3	■

HOW TO USE THIS BOOK

All mileage given is based on the latest records of the National Park Service. Figures may not coincide with those on park signposts that are outdated because of rerouted trails.

Hikers are encouraged to use the *Trails Illustrated Isle Royale National Park Map* published by the National Geographic Maps and sold in the park and through mail order by the Isle Royale & Keweenaw Parks Association (800-678-6925; *www.irkpa.org*).

Likewise, hikers should consult the most recent edition of the park's seasonal newspaper, *The Greenstone*, for changes in regulations and policy. This is available free by contacting Isle Royale National Park (906-482-0984; *www.nps.gov/isro*).

Directions in this book are given as if Isle Royale trends due east and west, strictly speaking, it is oriented northeast and southwest. Hikers, rangers, and the National Park Service speak of Windigo as being at the west end and Rock Harbor at the east end of the Island. To avoid confusion, this guide uses those directions.

Mapping Symbols

There are 35 maps in this edition of *Isle Royale National Park: Foot Trails & Water Routes*. The maps use the following symbols:

▲	Campground		Tower
	Ranger Station		Shipwreck
	Portage Marker		Lighthouse
▬	Dock	▲	Named Peak
	View Point	▲ 1102 ft	High Point
	Natural Attraction		Wetlands
	Waterfall	800	Contour Lines
✕	Mining Ruins	Mile 3.2	Mileage along the Trail
	Store	P 0.1 mi	Length of Portage

Isle Royale

The National Park

A backpacker along the Rock Harbor Trail near Three Mile Campground.

1   The Island and The Lady

As hard as I tried, I couldn't avoid it. On the second day of my Isle Royale adventure, I stood at Daisy Farm with plans of paddling the outside coast but instead watched Lake Superior's waves crash into Rock Harbor. The Lady was furious. So I paddled to the end of the harbor, threw the boat over my head, and began walking. Within a mile of the portage, my shoulders were throbbing from the grinding weight of the yoke. I stopped, lifted the boat to ease the pain, and there it was – once again – the red path.

On the trail from Moskey Basin to Lake Richie in Isle Royale National Park, you hike along a series of low rock outcroppings. In the middle of the woods, where the route cuts across the stone, there are no signs, no rock cairns, but also no question as to where you go. The massive boulders are gray, jagged, and covered with patches of green lichen. But the stone path across them is pink and so soft and smooth only the shuffle of thousands of boots could have laid this trail.

From Indians chasing game to miners looking for copper or even the padded paws of a wolf pack, historians and biologists can only guess who has followed this trail in the past. But one thing is certain. In the last half century it has been the rubber soles of what park officials technically term "backcountry users": visitors who hoist a pack or portage a canoe in an effort to experience perhaps the most dwindling resource in the world today – wilderness.

Myself included. I first walked the red path to Lake Richie in the early 1960s as a 9-year-old following his father on a day hike to catch pike. We caught none. But for a brief afternoon, we snuck away from the motorboats and bustling lodge at Rock Harbor to the edge of wilderness. The heart of the Island gripped my soul then and never let go. I returned in the 1970s as a backpacker and used the route to access the Greenstone Ridge Trail. In the 1980s I portaged a kayak across the red path, in the1990s I carried in a canoe. In the last few trips I returned to the simplicity of hauling only a backpack.

Six decades on the Island with each adventure a new challenge, each time carrying something different. But the trail never changed. It has always been the first portage and the final escape from the remaining vestiges of man and man's world in Rock Harbor. For myself and thousands of others each summer, the red path to Lake Richie is the threshold to the secluded wonder of the Island, the last barrier into a roadless, almost timeless place, forever preserved in the stormy northwest corner of Lake Superior.

Those are rare and valuable qualities in an age when our ability to lose ourselves in the woods is rapidly shrinking. Those are qualities that pull 18,000 visitors to Isle Royale every year. They begin arriving in mid-May; they are gone by late October. Come winter, Isle Royale is the only national park in the country to close down completely. No hikers, no tourists, no anglers, no hotel employees; empty except for a few researchers who keep tabs on the moose and wolves.

Some visitors plan their stay around the lodge at Rock Harbor. Others rarely step off their cabin cruisers, desiring only to fish offshore for lake trout. But the vast majority are backcountry users: day hikers, backpackers, canoeists, and kayakers. To them it is impossible to sit in a hotel room or on the deck of a boat and experience Isle Royale's richest offering. To enjoy the backcountry, they must travel to the backcountry. They seek the exhilaration of hauling a 35-pound pack over a new trail. They cherish a private encounter with a moose and her calf feeding in a beaver pond.

For those who desire this type of escape and vacation, the Island is well suited. Although small by National Park Service (NPS) standards, Isle Royale offers a greater variety of wilderness adventures than many parks twice its size. The Island is 45 miles long and 9 miles wide at its broadest point, comprising more than 210 square miles or 134,400 acres of wilderness. Its backbone, the Greenstone Ridge, climbs three times to more than 1300 feet, with Mount Desor the highest point at 1394 feet.

Spread across this area are 165 miles of trails, ranging from a well-defined hike along a level path to an up-and-down struggle over the Minong Ridge. You could arrange anything from a series of day hikes out of Rock Harbor to a 2-week trek that circles the park and never backtracks a single step. The vast majority of trails within the park are well marked and maintained with bridges, boardwalks, and walkways across wetlands and swamps. Not only do they keep your boots dry, but also they prevent the delicate marshes from turning into mud baths.

Or you can paddle. A series of portages connect nine lakes, with dozens of coves, harbors, bays, and isolated areas that neither hikers nor power boaters can reach. Canoeists have no fear of Lake Superior as they can route trips to stay completely in the sheltered security of the coves and inland lakes. Others embrace the lake known as the Lady. These are sea kayakers, who take to the outside coast of the park and marvel at the power of a 4-foot swell or the endless blue horizon the Lady has painted around the Island.

Day hikers, backpackers, canoeists, kayakers: Isle Royale offers them all a piece of her heart. You only need a desire to see land untrodden by man's heavy footprint. Leave the routines of the city behind and arrive prepared to experience the Island and the Lady on their terms.

Then follow a red path.

Isle Royale: History of a Wilderness

The Island was born during the Precambrian era, some 1.2 billion years ago when lava seeped up through cracks in the Superior Basin and formed basalt, the bedrock of the area. After each lava flow, wind and rain carried sand, gravel, and other sediments into the area, producing slabs of soft rock between the hard layers of basalt.

But the Island's distinct "washboard" appearance – ridges and valleys extending from one end of the park to the other – was formed when the center of the Superior Basin began to subside. This raised and tilted the layers of rocks on Isle Royale, the Keweenaw Peninsula, and much of the outer rim of the lake. The result was ridges with a steep northwest side and a gradual southeastern slope. Over thousands of years, the softer layers of sandstone eroded to form valleys and lakes. The bands of basalt withstood forces of nature to become the ridges that hikers struggle over every summer.

Glaciers added the final touch to Isle Royale's appearance. Four major ice sheets pushed their way down from Canada and scoured the land as far south as the Ohio River. The last glacier advanced to

A mining family at Windigo in the early 1890s (Fisher Collection, Michigan Technological University Archives).

the Lake Superior area only 11,000 years ago. When it melted, Isle Royale, as we know it today, appeared. The glacier's depressions on the land became lakes, coves, and harbors. The rock debris that it had scraped up and pulverized was left behind as a thin layer of soil. When the ice melted as the glacier retreated, the water filled Lake Superior.

Not long after the final glacier retreated, life appeared on the Island. Wind and water carried algae that took hold in wet places and lichens that could live on bare rock. Gradually, grass and other higher plants arrived and gained a foothold in the thin layer of glacial soil.

Grass and shrubs carpeted the barren ridges and prepared Isle Royale for the first animals. Birds and airborne insects easily reached the Island. A handful of caribou ventured across the frozen Lake Superior. Hawks, owls, and possibly even a few wolves soon left their home in Canada and were lured 15 miles southeast to the new land.

That was Isle Royale about 10,000 years ago: a sub arctic grassland with dwarfed birches and willows and wandering caribou. But as the climate continued to warm, the Island continued to change. Forests replaced the grasslands, and mammals such as beaver, snowshoe hare, and marten appeared along with amphibians, reptiles (such as the painted turtle), and various species of fish that thrived in the inland lakes.

But some animals never made the crossing from the Canadian mainland. Black bears, raccoons, porcupines, and white-tailed deer were notably missing.

Inevitably, man arrived. He had reached the north shore of Lake Superior by 7000 B.C. and could easily view the Island off in the distance. To the first Native Americans, Isle Royale was the "floating island" and had mystic qualities when the early morning fog made it appear to rise above the water.

We don't know when they made the 15-mile trip from Canada, but we have evidence that Indians were regularly mining copper by 2000 B.C. The metal was worth making the hazardous Lake Superior crossing. The Indians used a variety of beach cobbles to pound out the pure copper. They fashioned it into knives, bars, and beads that were traded as far away as New England and Mexico.

Although the Indians' activity peaked between 800 and 1600 B.C., it is believed that their settlements on Isle Royale were rare. Other than hundreds of shallow mining pits, the Native Americans left few signs of their habitation – unlike the Europeans who followed them to the Island.

Legends of pure copper reached white explorers late in the seventeenth century and prompted the French to explore western Lake Superior. The French gave the Island its formal name and included it on their earliest maps of the giant lake.

Benjamin Franklin may also have heard of the copper-rich island and insisted in the Treaty of Paris (1783) that the boundary between the fledgling United States and England's Canada be drawn north of Isle Royale. Other historians believe the United States ended up with the Island not through shrewd diplomacy but, rather, from a mapmaker's error that put the international boundary north of it. Although Isle Royale is much closer to Minnesota, Michigan was given control in 1837, when it became the first Lake Superior territory to be admitted to the Union.

Fishermen used the Isle Royale as early as 1800 and most likely were the first to simply call it "the Island" in the lake they referred to as "the Lady." Isle Royale was ideal for fishing, with its long shoreline, many reefs, and wide range of water depths that supported such desirable species as lake trout and whitefish. A small Indian fishing camp still remained at Belle Isle when the Northwest Fur Company sent fishermen to the north shore in the early 1800s.

In 1837, the American Fur Company built a fishing camp on Belle Isle and within 2 years had seven camps and a crew of 33 fishermen. The largest camp, on Siskiwit Bay, had a storehouse, salt house, a cooper's shop, and a barracks. When the company ceased operation in 1841 because of the economic depression of 1837-1841, fishing remained as an enterprise for individual fishermen.

For a short spell, fishing took a back seat to another enterprise. In 1844 the Chippewa Indians signed a treaty with the United States, giving up their claims to the land. That opened up the Island to full-scale prospecting for minerals. Miners arrived in three waves, with the first lasting from 1843 to 1855. The miners filed claims immediately after the treaty was signed and by 1846 had created a small copper rush to the Island. Although much exploration took place, little metal was ever obtained. The remains of two mines from this era can still be seen: Smithwick Mine, a fenced-in excavation on the Stoll Trail near Rock Harbor Lodge, and the Siskiwit Mine, a marked area on the Rock Harbor Trail between Three Mile and Daisy Farm campgrounds.

Crude mining methods and Isle Royale's isolation made it almost impossible for the numerous companies to turn a profit. By 1855 the last of them had ceased operating. But the demands of the Civil War raised the price of copper, and by 1873 there was new interest in what was beneath the rocky surface of Isle Royale.

This time there were fewer but better-financed companies using advanced techniques. Gone were the methods of finding copper veins by searching rock outcrops or burning away the underbrush. Instead, trained mining engineers and geologists used diamond drills to seek out the mineral. Reliable transportation in the form of lake steamers also aided the mining.

The result was several large mining adventures, including the largest at Minong Mine near McCargoe Cove. Hundreds of nearby Indian mining pits attracted the miners' interest in the ridge, and in 1875 they began to build a mining community. At its peak in the late 1870s, the Minong mining town was home for 154 workers and their families. It included a dock and warehouse at the mouth of McCargoe Cove for lake steamers, an office building, store, schoolhouse, and various houses. The miners also constructed a stamping mill, dam, and a railroad from the dock to the mine site that required a full-time blacksmith to shoe the horses used to pull the ore

A commercial fishery in Chippewa Harbor around 1892 (Fisher Collection, Michigan Technological University Archives).

cars and fabricate metal hardware.

Off of Siskiwit Bay was Island Mine, the site of the other major mining effort of the time. When 80 men reported to work in 1873, the Island Mining Company decided to lay out a township on the north side of the bay. They then built a 2-mile road from the bay to the inland mines. During the next few years, the company sank three shafts, one 200 feet deep, and constructed a sawmill, dock, and workers' quarters.

The two mines' prosperity, although short-lived, led to a demand of self-government among the workers. Isle Royale County was established in 1875 with Island Mine being the county seat and the Minong settlement a separate township. But poor deposits and falling copper prices ended another spell of mining in the early 1880s.

The final fling at mining occurred in 1889 when investors from England were persuaded to finance another search for profitable copper. This time they looked at the west end of the Island. The town of Ghyllbank was built at the present site of Windigo and included a two-story company building, storehouses, and sheds. The mining community numbered 135, including more than 20 children; two babies were born on the Island in the winter of 1890-1891. A second settlement was built 2 miles inland for workers and single men.

Although miles of roads were built (one as far east as Lake Desor) and extensive diamond drilling carried out, no copper of profitable quantities was ever found. Thus ended the mining era on Isle Royale,

Backpackers take a rest at the Siskowit Mine site along the Rock Harbor Trail.

a 4000-year stint that produced many artifacts and relics of man's existence – but little metal.

But commercial fishing had remained. It reached its peak in the 1880s with almost 30 fishing camps scattered along the shoreline, including a year-round settlement at Chippewa Harbor. But there was a noticeable drop in the number of whitefish caught in the late 1890s, and fishing began its decline. The creation of a national park in the 1940s hindered the industry, as rangers, enforcing the policy of the times, uprooted many fishermen who did not own land and burned their camps. Many fishermen had moved on anyway because of depressed fish prices, smaller catches, and opportunities to move to more profitable locations.

Disaster struck in 1952 when the first sea lamprey appeared in Lake Superior. The parasite, which attaches itself to a fish and sucks out the blood and body juices, almost wiped out the lake trout and drove most of the remaining licensed fishermen out of business. By 1972, though, the sea lampreys had been controlled. By then four fishing permits were left on the Island and today there is only one at Washington Island. The fishing industry, Isle Royale's most enduring commercial enterprise, still exists on Lake Superior, but is only a remnant of its glorious height in the late 1800s.

It was tourism that would blossom in the twentieth century. By

1870 a trickle of tourists arrived on excursion boats to picnic near the site of Siskiwit Mine or the Rock Harbor Lighthouse. But with the growth of Midwestern cities in the early 1900s, tourism on Isle Royale boomed. The Windigo Copper Company, unable to find any copper, began to mine tourists. Duluth businessmen built the exclusive Washington Club on the mainland, and Captain Singer of the White Transportation Line built Singer Resort, which featured a bowling alley and dance hall, on nearby Washington Island. Seven other resorts catering to passengers on the Great Lakes' steamers were built, including one on Belle Isle that boasted a fine dining room, shuffleboard courts, and even a pitch-and-putt golf course.

At the same time, people began to buy islands and plots of land for summer homes, particularly in Tobin Harbor. By 1920 the movement to turn the Island into a national park was underway. The man given most credit was journalist Albert Stoll, Jr. Stoll visited the Island in the 1920s and then wrote a series of articles for the Detroit News, promoting national park status for Isle Royale. Congress passed a bill in 1931 making Isle Royale a national park, and the federal government, by 1940, acquired all island lands.

Today Isle Royale is one of our smallest national parks and one of the most costly to visit. The special transportation needed to reach the Island and the numerous backpackers encourages visitors to stay longer and gives the park one of the longest visitation averages in the country. At Yellowstone National Park visits average only a few hours, but more than 4 days at Isle Royale.

It only seems right. People don't go to Isle Royale to sightsee but to escape. They want to experience the wilderness not merely see it like Old Faithful. To fully appreciate and understand Isle Royale, you must grab your paddle or your hiking boots and wander off for a week or more into the tranquility of its woods.

Only then will the shores of the Island beckon your return.

A highlight for many visitors to Isle Royale is encountering a moose.

2   Wildflowers to Wildlife

Early one February while working on the annual winter wolf count, biologists watched a male and female wolf and three pups enter a thicket near Lake Mason. Then to their utter amazement, they saw a moose run out of the trees followed by the male wolf lunging through the snow just inches away. Most kills occur at night, and for the scientists to actually witness this predator-prey relationship was a rare opportunity.

With a reckless leap, the male lunged through the air and locked his jaws on the back leg of the running moose. Hanging on was a near-impossible task, and one biologist would later write that the animal appeared to be "flopping like a rag doll" in midair. But when the moose slowed to weave through another stand of trees, the female seized the opportunity, and now there were two wolves, attached leechlike, to the hindquarters. The moose quickly collapsed onto its sternum but kept its head up while the wolves tore at its rump, turning the white snow deep red. Suddenly the moose lunged forward, regained its feet, and thrashed the still-clinging male with rapid-fire kicks with its other rear leg. At the same time, it lashed out at the female as she danced just out of reach in front. The attack was now in a frenzied peak with the blood-soaked male refusing to let go and the moose whirling back and forth in an effort to trample the female.

Unable to gain a grip anywhere else, the female again attached herself to the other rear quarter. Now the wolves were dragged, side-by-side, over logs and thrown against trees as the moose whirled around. But the wolves held on and eventually the moose went down on its sternum again. For a while the moose sat up, panted heavily, and glanced at the predators tearing at its hindquarters. But gradually its lungs became feeble, the rear legs would no longer kick, and inevitably it collapsed into the snow.

Life and death on Isle Royale.

The Island is truly...an island. The expanse of Lake Superior has given it both solitude and protection. From wildflowers to wildlife, Isle Royale has endured the modern world. Despite man's appearance, life on the Island still turns in its natural cycles. There is harmony between plants and animals, between predators and prey, between life and death. Man visits and occasionally rearranges a few pieces, but never has he changed the rules of the game.

This is what makes Isle Royale unique: an absence of outside influence on the behavior of animals and plants. The natural barrier of Lake Superior hinders most immigration and emigration of additional species. The Island also has fewer species than the mainland. Many animals never made the crossing after the last glacier scraped the Island clean 10,000 years ago.

Add man's own dedication not to interfere with the natural cycles, and you have animals and plants that behave and live in the most pristine manner. You have the perfect outdoor laboratory.

The Fauna

Much of the research that takes place on the Island revolves around the wolf. Unlike its other habitats in northern Minnesota or Michigan's Upper Peninsula, on Isle Royale the wolf is controlled not by man's encroaching presence but by its own social behavior and the availability of moose – its food source during much of the year.

The wolves strengthen the moose herd by helping to thin out those unable to survive the harsh winter – the old, the sick, and the young. It's an ancient predator-prey cycle. But a strong adult moose has little to fear from a pack of wolves. Its flashing hoofs are protection enough. Thus, the size and condition of the moose herd help determine the growth of the wolf packs.

Other factors – alternate food supplies, weather, and the mortality rate of the newborn – also play a hand in the survival of each species. But there is little doubt that one without the other would create havoc on the Island.

This was proven at the turn of the century and again in the late 1980s. Faced with growing competition for food on the mainland,

An Isle Royale wolf pack in winter (Dr. Rolf Peterson photo).

the first moose swam to Isle Royale around 1900. Here the moose found an abundance of shrubs and no natural predators. The new herd exploded in numbers, and by 1930 an estimated 3000 moose lived on the Island.

The herd began to fluctuate wildly. In the winter of 1933, a large number starved to death. The great fire of 1936, which burned 20 percent of the Island, created vast open areas for small trees and shrubs to take root. The new source of "moose salad" caused another upswing in population.

The boom-and-bust pattern might have continued, but nature finally brought a predator to the Island. In 1948, a few wolves crossed the 15-mile ice bridge from the mainland and found a ready food supply. Within 8 years, an estimated 15 to 25 wolves lived in the park. In 1967, several more wolves, with fur that was distinctively darker than that of wolves already on the Island, had made the Lake Superior crossing.

Researchers believed that the moose and wolf predator-prey relationship fluctuated within a cycle with the increase in one species causing a delayed increase in the other. But in 1980 the cycle fell out of sync. That year the wolves on the Island reached an all-time high of 50 animals in five territorial packs. Just 2 years later, the number had dropped to 14, with only 4 of them traveling in a pack. The wolves rebounded to more than 20 in 1984 and then began a 5-year decline. When the population dropped to 12, wildlife biologists feared the days of the eastern timber wolf on Isle Royale were numbered.

Up to that point, scientists had watched the wolves and counted them in annual winter surveys but never interfered with the packs. Then, changing its "hands-off" policy, the NPS approved a plan that allowed researchers to live-capture the wolves for the first time to take blood samples and place radio collars on seven of them.

The problem, many biologists believed, was not disease or a shortage of food but a lack of genetic variability. There were so few wolves on the Island that inbreeding had resulted and the reproductive rate of the packs had dropped. "They're not so much dying as they're just not reproducing," said one park researcher. But the

Loons at Isle Royale

No other animal, not even the moose or a wolf, exemplifies the north woods like the common loon. Its eerie, demented laugh and distinctive checkered back is synonymous to many backpackers and paddlers with pure water, quiet lakes and unmarred wilderness.

An adult loon is a large, long-bodied bird with a wingspan of close to five feet and a weight that occasionally tops 15 pounds. During the summer its trademark features are easy to spot: a black head, red eye and broken white collar. Loons appear awkward when taking off and landing. They thrash along the surface of a lake for up to 100 yards before finally becoming airborne and often slam hard into the water when landing.

But under the lake they are almost unmatched in their ability to swim and dive. Loons have been snared in nets up to 180 feet below the surface of a lake and have been clocked in dives lasting 15 minutes. Their large web feet, placed at the rear of their streamlined bodies, are almost useless on land but in the water are rudder-like paddles that allow them to dive in an instant and swim fast enough to spear a 6-inch trout.

Isle Royale has the most stable common loon population in Michigan, where the bird is listed as a "threatened species." The Island also has the only known loon population that uses Great Lakes waters, as opposed to inland lakes, for nesting. Park researchers have recorded adult loons on 27 of the 47 inland lakes and in 37 of the 45 Lake Superior sites where they have known to nest in the past.

As intriguing as loons are to watch, backcountry visitors, especially paddlers, have to be extremely careful about not distributing them. Research has shown that loons are very vulnerable to any kind of human disturbance particularly while nesting. The nesting period is from late April to early July and if a loon is driven off its nest the eggs or chicks are left exposed to predators or even abandon-

wolves of Isle Royale rebounded in the 1990s and in the winter of 1998-1999 recorded their greatest documented increase, from 14 to 25 animals in three packs. In 2009 there were 24 wolves in four packs.

If you have arrived to see a wolf, chances are you will leave Isle Royale disamer, the wolves turn to beaver as well as moose for their food source; they stay in the isolated sections of the park, avoid-

ment. Since 1997, park researchers have documented at least three incidents where boating activity – both power boaters and paddlers – contributed to the abandonment of a nest with chicks in it.

It's important that visitors to Isle Royale do their part to help protect the Island's fragile loon population.

Know the signs of a threatened or distressed loon. A loon alters its behavior when you are too close. The bird may move away, sink low in the water, frantically flap its wings, give a tremolo call, or repeatedly dive around your boat. Loons are best observed with binoculars from a distance of at least 100 yards. Do not chase them in your canoe!

During the incubation period from late May to early July avoid small islands and protected coves. If you see a loon on shore it is most likely incubating eggs. Leave the area as quickly as possible! If you see it crouched low with its head down, it is likely feeling threatened. If you see the loon slip into the water, you have scared it off its nest.

From late June through August watch for adult loons with chicks. For the first few weeks, loon chicks are small fluff balls of black downy feathers and then gradually change their color to a more subdued gray and white. It is critical that canoers and kayakers steer well clear of an adult loon swimming with chicks.

ing almost all contact with people. If camping or hiking around the Feldtmann Lake area, you can often spot their tracks in the nearby swamps. And a small number of visitors will hear them howl at night, an eerie bark that is rarely forgotten. Despite all the trails that crisscross the Island, the wolf still has its solitude on Isle Royale.

The moose population has also fluctuated wildly at times. In 1977, less than 600 moose lived on the Island. By 1987, with the decrease in wolves, the herd had grown to more than 1600 and in the mid-1990s hit a peak of almost 2500. But in 2004 the herd began a steady decrease that many believe is the result of global warming and rising temperatures. The warm, dry weather of summer allows winter ticks to flourish and infest the moose, one of the main reasons the Isle Royale herd has declined to 530 animals in 2009.

Still you have a much better opportunity to spot moose in the Island's backcountry than a wolf. The ungainly animal, which can exceed a height of 7 feet and weigh more than 1000 pounds, is not skittish and tolerate people quite well. Often after encountering a hiker on a trail, a cow will take a few seconds to study the intruder before casually departing the area. During the rutting, from mid-September to late October, bulls have been known to keep backpackers awake with their constant snorting late into the night.

In the summer, moose feed on white birch and aspen in the forest and aquatic plants in streams, lakes, and beaver ponds. Small aspens, stripped of every leaf and branch, line the trails and are an indication that a bull could be feeding around the next bend.

Although you could spot one virtually anywhere, even at Rock Harbor Lodge, they seem to frequent Lake Richie, Feldtmann Lake, Lake Whittlesey, and Grace Creek. Feldtmann Lake Campground is a good spot to spend a night or two to view moose, whereas Washington Creek might be the easiest place to see one. During the calving season, a few cows with their newborn often seek the human activity at Washington Creek Campground because they know the area will be free of wolves.

Park rangers warn visitors that the moose should be treated with caution and never molested--especially the bulls, which can be temperamental during the summer and during rutting season in the fall. Many experienced backpackers rate the moose as the most dangerous animal in North America and the source of even more unpleasant confrontations than the bear.

Visitors should avoid upsetting any wildlife in the park, disturbing or touching their homes or nests, or disrupting their daily activities. The worst thing a backpacker can do is feed any animal, even a camp fox. This only upsets the balance of their natural food chain and makes them dependent on man and his leftovers.

But viewing wildlife is often the highlight of any trip, and one creature you can watch for hours is the beaver. Found in large numbers on the Island, the beaver's handiwork affects almost every species and drastically changes Isle Royale's landscape. The ponds the animals create are a source of food for the moose but destroy habitat for others. The wolves look for beaver lodges for nourishment in the summer, and paddlers will curse the dams when they have to drag their canoe over one coming from Chickenbone Lake to McCargoe Cove.

An estimated 1900 beavers inhabited the park in the mid-1970s, and today their distinctive lodges can still be seen along many trails. The lodges are built of sticks and mud and usually house a breeding pair and three or four young. In the summer they feed on aquatic and leafy vegetation, but during the rest of the year they turn to twigs and the inner bark of aspen and birch.

A beaver will let you know when you have paddled into its territory on an inland lake. The animal will approach your boat to within 5 or 6 feet and then slap the water with its tail as it dives below. When done unsuspectingly from behind, it's enough to make you drop your paddle.

During their stay hikers will also spot red foxes, even if they hike no farther than Daisy Farm Campground. In recent years, the carnivore has become used to man, and now every campground seems to have its own "camp fox" making daily rounds for handouts. In the wild the fox feeds on squirrels, hares, fish, and berries and often during the winter scavenges on the remains of wolf-killed moose. Foxes can be a nuisance in the backcountry because they rummage through packs and supplies left outside the tent at night. More than one hiker has awakened in the morning to find his or her food spread over the campground. For this reason, park rangers recommend that food be stored in Ziploc bags and covered with tarps and sticks or hung in a tree as if you were in bear country. They also warn not to feed foxes, which thereby become more dependent on humans. Other commonly seen mammals are hares and red squirrels. There are also mink, otter, muskrat, and various species of bats on the Island but are harder to spot.

The western painted turtle and the common garter snake are usually the only reptiles hikers spot. The most common amphibians in the park are the American toad, the spring peeper tree frog, and the green frog.

Because they are so mobile, a variety of birds can be found in the park – more than any other vertebrate – and encounters with them are inevitable. The most captivating, especially for canoeists and kayakers, is the loon. The common loon, with its distinctive laugh, can be heard throughout the Island and almost every lake seems to have a pair that can be viewed on a quiet evening in the backcountry.

Other waterfowl that will be seen frequently are the Canada goose, mallard, American black duck, bufflehead, and the distinctive common and red-breasted merganser. Isle Royale also has an abundance of woodpecker, chickadees, warblers, thrushes, kingfishers, and various species of gulls. Along the shoreline, the herring gull is the predominate species, but an occasional ring-billed gull can also be seen.

The Flora

It's the trees that hikers study the most on Isle Royale. Thick forests blanket the Island from Windigo to Blake Point and are broken up only by scattered lakes, swamps, and stretches of rocky ridges. The trees vary in density and variety, but they are always there, crowding the trail and shielding the wildlife community.

Forests on the Island, like wildlife, grow in cycles. When fire or wind creates new open areas in the vegetation, the first seedlings to take root are paper birch, aspen, and, sometimes, jack pine and various willows. These trees can tolerate the warm and usually drier growing conditions to form a successional forest.

If the seedlings are not over-browsed by moose, the forest will grow quickly and create a thick canopy, shading the ground. Paper birch and aspen seedlings find it hard to survive in the new conditions, but other trees do not, and they form the climax forests that gradually replace the successional ones.

The modifying effect of Lake Superior creates the ideal conditions for the first climax forest. The lake water keeps the summers cool and the winters mild along the shore. White spruce and balsam-fir seedlings find these cool, moist, and shaded surroundings ideal. Spruce-fir climax forest exists along the periphery of the park

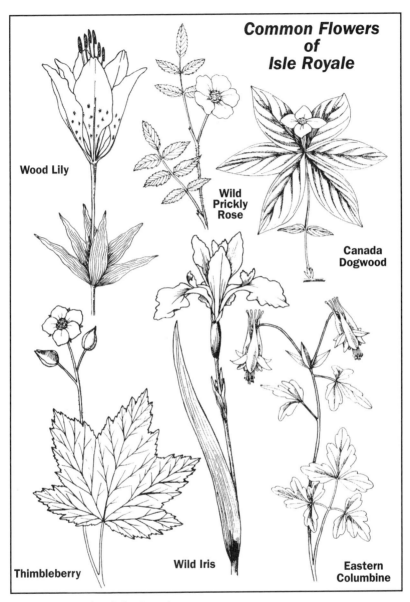

**Common Flowers
of
Isle Royale**

Wood Lily

Wild
Prickly
Rose

Canada
Dogwood

Thimbleberry

Wild Iris

Eastern
Columbine

and over much of the interior.

Inland, where ridges break up the terrain, the climate is warmer and drier than that along the shore. These conditions support a climax forest of sugar maple and yellow birch. The tops of Mount Desor and Sugar Mountain (hence its name) are almost pure stands of sugar maple, and maple-birch forests range inland a few miles out of Windigo along the Greenstone Ridge, past Ishpeming Point.

When a destructive force such as wind or fire again destroys part of the climax forest, the cycle is completed. The new open areas attract aspen and paper-birch seedlings, and a successional forest takes root,

In-between the two climax forests are transition zones, where yellow birch, jack pine, or aspen is dominant. In swamps and bogs, black spruce and northern white cedar thrive.

The best way to see and understand the park's succession of trees is to hike the Island Mine Trail from Siskiwit Campground. The trail begins at the western end of the bay in cool, moist, spruce-fir climax forest, dips into swamps of white cedar and black spruce, and then gradually climbs through a transition forest of spruce, fir, maple, and yellow birch. Eventually, the trail ends at the top of the Greenstone Ridge, where mostly sugar maple and yellow birch can be found.

Hikers along the trails spend most of their time looking at trees. But it is the wildflowers that catch their eye and break the green monotony of the forest. The wildflowers on the Island are incredible. An official park publication lists 101 kinds, most of which bloom later in the summer than those on the mainland.

Flowers also tend to bloom first at the west end of the park (at Windigo) and then gradually ripple eastward toward Rock Harbor. When hiking in late June and early July, backpackers heading east are often blessed with a rainbow of flowers along the trails.

The most impressive display of wildflowers occurs in open areas, where tree seedlings do not crowd out late bloomers such as the wood lily. In swamps, it is common to see the purple wild iris, large skunk cabbage, yellow pond lily, or white wild calla.

On the ridges, the hiker will encounter massive growths of western thimbleberry with its white flower, reddish wild prickly rose, or white upright bindweed, also known as the dwarf morning glory.

In the forest is the common Canada dogwood, American starflower, and the hard-to-find yellow lady's slipper. The most common berries are blueberries, dwarf raspberries, thimbleberries, and strawberries.

3 Wilderness Fishing

I was watching my silver and red spoon flutter through the wilderness waters of Lake Richie when my attention was diverted – a loon appeared. Not more than 50 yards away there was that distinctive black head bobbing on the lake and the accompanying eerie laugh.

The loon captivated me, they always do, so I missed that dark figure when it emerged from a patch of pencil reeds beneath the water and lunged at the flashing silver of my lure passing by. The strike almost made me fall out of the canoe. At one point the lake was smooth and still and I was casually listening to the call of the north woods. The next second I was yanking on my rod with a northern pike exploding out of the water.

"Gotcha!"

This one was so big that my first concern wasn't landing the fish but losing my tackle. When traveling through the backcountry of the Island, when everything you need must either fit into a canoe or be stuffed into a backpack, there's no room for the pile of lures, rods, and reels that's forever stashed in the trunk of the car. I had one backpacking rod that broke down into five pieces, a small reel that held only 6-pound test line, and 10 lures for 2 weeks. Losing this silver and red spoon would be the equivalent on any other trip to dropping the top tray of my tackle box in the water. So the drag was turned to one of its lighter settings, and when the big pike ran there was little I could do but watch it and wait to work some line in.

Eventually, monofilament won out: the fish tired and I gently picked it out of the lake--a 28-inch northern pike. Not bad. Neither were the filets and the shoreline feast after several days of dining on dinners that come in small foil pouches and, depending on how patient your stomach was, either had the crunch of Grape Nuts or the consistency of Cream-O-Wheat.

Wilderness fishing – there are some of us who believe angling doesn't get any better than this. The scenery is excellent, the passing wildlife is plentiful, and you can often have a lake to yourself. And when you do catch a fish, it's much more appreciated than the planned menu of chicken-a-la-king and cup-a-soup.

The only requirements are wilderness with lakes and a willingness to portage a boat or hike a trail. Bring a rod and a handful of lures and the Island will supply the rest. Only a dozen of the 47 inland lakes do not contain sport fish; the rest support such species as lake, brook, and rainbow trout, yellow perch, walleye, pumpkinseed sunfish, and, of course, pike, the most widespread game fish, thriving in 29 of the park's lakes.

Although Isle Royale has always been noted for its lake trout fishery offshore, which draws an annual migration of power boaters, the number of lines dipped into the lakes is relatively few in comparison. Two natural barriers keep the anglers limited and the action good. The first is Lake Superior. The fact that you can't drive to the park and fish 20 yards from your car has always kept the number of anglers down.

The second barrier is the inland lakes themselves, both their inaccessibility and the fact that no motors are allowed on them. Once on the Island, there is no shortcut to reach them, only the traditional way--on foot. Once on the lake the only way to travel is by paddle. That, more than anything, will always ensure light fishing pressure within the park.

Shore fishing from the trails is productive but restrictive in the number of lakes you can get to and the amount of water you can work. The best way to fish the inland lakes is to portage a boat in – no easy task. The most common boat in the park is the canoe, although others prefer to pack-in a small, two-man rubber raft, a belly boat, or even a kayak.

No matter what is used, you first have to carry it in before you can paddle it out. The system of 17 portages ranges from a 75-yard hop, skip, and a jump at Pickerel Cove to a 2.1-mile haul between Moskey Basin at the end of Rock Harbor to Lake Richie. Some backpackers prefer to carry a canoe in pairs but that is awkward at best.

A Lake Richie northern pike.

The most common method, for either canoe or kayak, is to attach a yoke over the top and flip it upside down on the shoulders of one person. With your head deep inside, you struggle down the trail, balancing the boat and bumping the trees.

Few people can go more than a half mile without giving their shoulders and back an extended rest. Even fewer people are lucky enough to carry their boat and gear in one trip. Portaging means returning to the original departing point for a second trip to haul what was left behind.

At times portaging is work, at times it is a grunt. But the results are being able to fish sections of the park that hikers can't get to-and pike, a lake trout, or walleye sizzling in a pool of butter at dinner time.

Lake Richie is often the first stop for backpacking anglers on Isle Royale. The deep lake, one or two days' travel from Rock Harbor Lodge, supports large populations of pike and yellow perch. Hikers can follow a trail around the northern edge of the lake and reach many weed beds where pike like to hide out.

But those who haul a boat over the trail have the entire lake to fish. The best spots in Richie tend to be the patches of weeds in the small bays along the shore, between the islets, and lining the southern arm that leads off to Chippewa Harbor. Use spoons or large bucktail spinners of almost any color and cast among the weeds and marshes. Use a fast retrieve and be ready. Pike often follow the spoon right to the side of the boat or the shoreline before taking the lure with a smashing strike.

Siskiwit Lake, the largest (with a length of 7 miles and a depth of

142 feet), contains the best variety of sport fish. A water-taxi service (see chapter 4) will take you to Malone Bay Campground, an easy 0.2-mile portage from Siskiwit. The large lake contains populations of perch, rainbow trout, and pike while many of the streams emptying into it can be stalked for brook trout. Some of the best pike habitat is found around and in Wood Lake, which can be reached from Siskiwit without a portage.

But Siskiwit's most prized catch is lake trout, some as large as 10 pounds, as it contains the only inland population of the fish. Like in Lake Superior, deepwater trolling is the most productive method to land a laker, and some backpackers have actually carried in small, portable downriggers in an attempt to get their spoons near the bottom. Others simply paddle across the lake with additional lead or a bottom bouncer-type sinker attached to their line. Come in early May or early June and the lake trout are often found within 3 or 4 feet of the surface before the heat of July sends them to the depths of Siskiwit.

Chickenbone, Livermore, and LeSage are a series of lakes in the central part of the park that have excellent foot and portage access

Fishing The Lady from a Kayak

Along with the usual spare paddle, bilge pump and dry bags, an increasing number of kayakers are arriving at Isle Royale with a rod and reel. As they paddle Lake Superior, weaving through the maze of rocky reefs and tiny islets that characterizes the Island's shoreline, they figure they might as well throw a line in.

The most effective way for kayakers to catch dinner is trolling, pulling their lure 25 to 50 feet behind them as they paddle through Isle Royale's many coves and channels. The natural speed of most kayakers is often an ideal trolling speed for catching coho salmon, lake trout and northern pike, the prime species anglers target in Lake Superior. Many anglers will equip their kayaks with rod holders so they can paddle unobtrusively. The even more serious might mount a fish finder device so they can read depths or locate underwater structure.

Although it's possible to catch lake trout and salmon close to the surface, and certainly a pike, often during the summer the most productive fishing is in deeper waters. Kayaks rely on deep diving crank baits to seek out fish in 10 to 15 feet of water. For deeper water they will attach a diver, the best known is *Dipsey Diver*, on their line and are popular with backpacking anglers, especially Chickenbone, because foot trails follow much of its west end, part of the north end, and touch a section of the south side. All three are productive spots for pike and perch, and Chickenbone also boasts walleye.

But if it's walleye you're eyeing, the best destination is Lake Whittlesey. Getting to the lake is not easy, the reason it's not heavily fished. One route includes two long portages in paddling to the western end of Chippewa Harbor and then a 0.5-mile portage into Whittlesey; the other is to paddle and portage in from Wood Lake.

For backcountry anglers, walleyes are usually a more challenging fish to catch than pike or perch. The most popular technique is vertical-jigging with an I/8- to 1/4-ounce jig that has been tipped with a rubber grub body, more commonly known as a Twister Tail. Vertical-jigging is merely bouncing the jig down the slope or along the bottom in a slow presentation. Search the lake for underwater gravel bars, shoreline bluffs, or wherever a steep rocky slope might attract and hold walleye.

Keep in mind that walleye are light sensitive and that most strikes come at dawn and dusk. Also remember that the strike of a

Kayakers paddle towards the entrance of Rock Harbor.

that will take their lures and spoons below the surface to depths of 20, 30, 40 feet or more.

Some of the best places for kayakers to troll are the mouths of Moskey Basin, Chippewa Harbor and McCargoe Cove or any of the coves in the Five Fingers region of the park but particularly Belle Harbor. Keep in mind that you must have a Michigan fishing license to fish Lake Superior and all connecting bays and coves.

walleye is more of a light tap, not brutal lunges with which the pike of Lake Richie spoiled you. If not equipped to cast for walleyes, take heart. There are also northern pike in Lake Whittlesey.

From mid- to late summer, after the loons are done nesting, Isle Royale also offers the ultimate in wilderness fishing: casting into a lake with no trail or portage leading to it, no access at all other than cross-country travel with a compass in hand. This is the most challenging adventure in angling, and often you go unrewarded after spending a morning bashing through the trees. Just the idea that you'll have a lake to yourself or might be the only person to fish it that summer is enough to pull some of us off the trail.

The opportunities for angling adventures of this nature are only limited by your imagination and skill with a compass or GPS unit. Lake Halloran, located off the Feldtmann Ridge Trail and 2 miles west of Siskiwit Bay Campground, is said to have some "monster pike," while one backpacker told me that Lake Eva, a short climb from Pickerel Cove, was a hot spot for walleye. Then there is Sargent Lake with its many coves and islets. I've always wondered how many people have fished that large body of water. All three lakes support nesting loons and cross-country anglers should not attempt to reach them until after mid-July.

The most successful off-trail anglers are the ones who not only find the remote bodies of water but also make provisions to get beyond the shoreline, where often the numerous deadheads or thick weeds make casting a nightmare.

Canoes are usually too bulky and large to portage off-trail, making inflatable rafts or belly boats a much wiser choice. If hauling that kind of gear isn't accommodating to the rest of your itinerary, consider packing a pair of lightweight waders that can be worn with an old pair of tennis shoes.

A fishing license is not needed for the inland lakes – only for Lake Superior, which falls under the jurisdiction of the State of Michigan. You can purchase a 24-hour license at the concession stores in Rock Harbor or Windigo or any license in advance online from the Michigan Department of Natural Resources and Environment (*www. michigan.gov/dnre*).

If you do land a fish and decide to keep it, be sure to properly dispose of the remains. Rock Harbor has a fish-cleaning station, while in Windigo the rangers ask anglers to place the remains in a plastic bag and dispose of them in the trash cans near the visitors center. In the backcountry, cut the remains into pieces smaller than 4 inches and puncture the air bladders. Then dispose of them either in Lake Superior where the water is deeper than 50 feet or in deep water in an inland lake via a canoe if possible. Never dispose of fish remains near campgrounds, docks, or trails because in recent years wolves have been sighted near these areas looking for what successful anglers leave behind. This is a bad situation for both wolves and people.

Only artificial lures may be used on the inland lakes of Isle Royale; live, dead or preserved bait is prohibited. In 2009, the NPS also instituted a barbless-hook-only regulation for all inland lakes, streams and creeks. Arrive with single barbless hooks or bend down the barbs on the hooks if they have them.

Know the minimum size limits for the species of fish you are targeting. All brook trout, whose populations are dangerously low, are catch-and-release only for all inland lakes and streams and Lake Superior 4.5 miles out from the island. Keep only the fish you plan to eat and release all others as quickly as possible. Carry along a pair of needle-nose pliers or hemostats to quickly remove a hook from a fish and try to release them without removing them from the water. Finally the NPS urges all anglers to avoid using split shot made of lead, as the ingestion of them is toxic to loons and other waterfowl.

Even if you don't have much fishing experience, or any at all, pack along a small outfit if you are planning a paddling trip to the Island. A 6-foot, two-piece graphite rod, equipped with an open-face reel and 6- or 8-pound test line is ideal. Take a handful of spoons, such as Daredevils and Little Cleos ranging from 1/2- to 3/4-ounce, along with some large spinners, like No. 3 Mepps. Then in the evenings, quietly paddle along the lake casting and quickly retrieving the lures at the edge of weed patches, deadheads, or even beaver dams and lodges, any place where a pike might be hiding in shallow water. You might not catch a fish or even get a strike, but a rod and reel gives you a good excuse to be out on the water in the evening when a lake can be so still it reflects shoreline pines and the air so quiet you can hear a mayfly overhead.

Fish often enough and some night, when a moose appears or a beaver swims by and your mind has wandered in the wilderness, when you least expect it... "Gotcha!"

The Voyageur II *drops off backpackers at McCargoe Cove Campground.*

4 Getting To & Around The Island

We scrambled to the outdoor decks of the *Ranger III* to watch the center span of the historic Houghton-Hancock Lift Bridge rise high into the air. We waved at people onshore along the Keweenaw Waterway, a part natural, part man-made canal across the Keweenaw Peninsula, and they waved back. We talked excitedly with each other about our upcoming trip at Isle Royale National Park.

Then we entered the blue.

When the National Park Service boat reaches the open water of Lake Superior the lively excitement onboard is replaced by quiet contemplation. With the exception of an occasional seagull or a passing freighter, the only thing we can see for the next four hours is the endless blue horizon of the world's largest freshwater lake. Everybody on board is hypnotized by the power, coldness and overwhelming size of Lake Superior.

Then somebody spots a thin green line to the north and with every passing wave we watch it slowly emerge as an island with trees, a lighthouse and a craggy shoreline of bluffs and coves. When we finally reach our destination, Rock Harbor, the national park's main entry point, we are a world away from our mundane routines at home, free from work, PTA meetings, rush-hour traffic and – this place is so remote – even email and text messages.

Islands – it's how you escape in the Great Lakes.

There are two ways to arrive at Isle Royale – by air or by water. You can jump on a small floatplane in Houghton and be at the park in 30 minutes. But there is something special about making the crossing by boat and watching Isle Royale grow from a thin dark line on the horizon to a rocky shoreline of towering pines. By experiencing Lake Superior first, you later gain a sense of Isle Royale's solitude and isolation. The Lady awakens you to the wilderness that she has preserved throughout time.

You never gain a feeling for the lake by flying over it. And when you land, you arrive at just another national park. Lake Superior is Isle Royale; it surrounds the Island, protects it, gives it the mystic charm that has always lured men and animals across to it.

Getting There

Although Ranger III is the most well-known vessel that travels to the Island, several others make the trip from different departure

Re-supplying at Isle Royale

During a lengthy trip in Isle Royale's backcountry many visitors would rather not be packing along all their supplies. This is particularly true for backpackers, as carrying food, even freeze-died packets, for a week or longer makes for an extremely heavy pack.

One solution is to arrange a food drop-off through the U.S. Post Office, utilizing its designated carrier, the *Voyageur II*. You can mail a package to yourselves to either Windigo or Rock Harbor and then meet the boat to receive it. Fuel cannot be sent through the U.S. Mail and plan on your package arriving a day or two prior to your delivery date. When mailing yourself a package write your destination (Windigo or Rock Harbor) and date of pick-up (month, day and year) on the lower left side and address it to: Your Name, c/o Voyageur II, Grand Portage, MN 55605.

The *Voyageur II* circumnavigates the island after arriving at Windigo and for a fee will also drop-off packages at McCargoe Cove, Belle Isle, Daisy Farm, Chippewa Harbor, Malone Bay or Windigo. Make prior arrangements with the ferry company for this service.

Finally if all you want is a clean shirt for after the long hike, hand deliver a package to the Rock Harbor Lodge or the Windigo Store. Both will store extra supplies for a fee.

For more information contact Forever Resorts (866-644-2003), Rock Harbor Lodge (906) 337-4993), the Grand Portage- Isle Royale Transportation Line (888-746-2305, 218-475-0024; *www.isleroyale-boats.com*) or the Grand Portage Post Office (218-475-2303).

points. Water transportation is available from Houghton and Copper Harbor, Michigan, and Grand Portage, Minnesota, the closest of the three.

Ranger III is a government-operated ship that measures 165 feet and carries 126 passengers and pleasure boats up to 20 feet in length. It is the largest vessel operating between Isle Royale and the mainland, and rarely do rough seas prevent her from making the trip. On board is a snack bar, viewing lounges, and an NPS ranger who conducts interpretation programs, helps backpackers with trip plans, and fills out back-country permits for hikers eager to start their wilderness experience the minute they arrive.

Ranger III begins its season in late May and finishes in mid-September. Operating days and dates vary slightly from year to year for all vessels. *Ranger III* departs Houghton at 9:00 A.M. on Tuesdays and Fridays from the dock in front of the NPS headquarters and arrives at Rock Harbor Lodge around 3:00 P.M. It overnights at Rock Harbor before returning to Houghton the following day.

It is wise to get reservations on *Ranger III* or any of the ships. For the NPS boat, reservations can be made starting in January, Monday through Friday during normal office hours at the park headquarters. Full fare must be paid in advance. You can now make book reservations for the *Ranger III* online through the Isle Royale web site at *www.nps.gov/isro.*

For more information or to make reservations by phone or mail, contact:

Isle Royale National Park
800 E. Lakeshore Dr.
Houghton, MI 49931
(906) 482-0984; Fax (906) 482-8753

By traveling northeast along the Keweenaw Peninsula, you can cut the sailing time by 1.5 hours. From Copper Harbor at the very tip of the peninsula, the 100-foot *Isle Royale Queen IV* departs for a 3-hour trip to the park.

The 100-passenger ship, put into service in 2005, begins its season in mid-May and completes its last trip in late September. In May and after Labor Day, it leaves Copper Harbor Monday and Friday only for Rock Harbor Lodge. Once arriving at the park the boat turns around and on the same day returns to Copper Harbor. In the first two weeks of June it departs on Monday, Wednesday, Friday and Saturday and in July the vessel leaves Copper Harbor daily except

Wednesday. In August it makes the round-trip run to Isle Royale daily. The boat always departs Copper Harbor at 8:00 A.M. and Rock Harbor Lodge at 2:45 P.M. the same day.

There is food service on board. A full deposit is required and reservations are strongly recommended and can be made year-round. For more information check the Isle Royale Line web site at *www. isleroyale.com*. To make reservations contact:

The Isle Royale Line
P.O. Box 24
Copper Harbor, MI49918-0024
(906) 289-4437; Fax (906) 289-4952

Two privately owned ferries depart from Grand Portage for the 1.5 to 2-hour trip to the park. Both stop at Windigo, the ranger station at the western end of the Island.

From mid-June to early September the 65-foot *Wenonah* departs Wednesday, Friday and Saturday from Grand Portage at 8:30 A.M. (Central Daylight Time) and then returns from Windigo the same day at 2 P.M . (Central Daylight Time). From mid-July to mid-August it also sails on Thursday and Sunday at the same times.

The other vessel out of Grand Portage is the 63-foot *Voyageur II*. The boat runs from early May to late October. From late May to late September, it departs Grand Portage Monday, Wednesday and Saturday at 7:30 A.M. (Central Daylight Time), stops at Windigo, and overnights at Rock Harbor Lodge. The following day, Tuesday, Thursday and Sunday, it departs from Rock Harbor at 8 A.M. (Central Daylight Time) for Windigo and Grand Portage. For most of May the ship departs Grand Portage only on Wednesday and Saturday and mid-September through mid-October only on Wednesday, Saturday and Sunday.

Reservations for *Wenonah* and *Voyageur II* are taken year-round, and full deposit is required. For more information on both vessels, check the Grand Portage – Isle Royale Transportation Line web site at *www.isleroyaleboats.com*. To make reservations contact:

Grand Portage – Isle Royale Transportation Line
P.O. Box 10529
White Bear Lake, Minnesota 55110
Phone (651) 653-5872 or (888)746-2305
May thru Oct (218) 475-0024 or (218) 475-0074

Regularly scheduled seaplane service is available out of Houghton for either Windigo or Rock Harbor Lodge. Many backpackers take advantage of the service by taking the plane to Windigo, hiking to Rock Harbor Lodge, and returning on the Ranger III

Royale Air Service provides on-demand service from mid-May to mid-September, often flying to the park Monday through Saturday during the summer. Flights depart from the Houghton County Airport and land in the protected bays at Windigo and Rock Harbor. The amphibious Cessna 206 carries up to four passengers along with 50 pounds of gear per person.

Full payment is required when you make your reservation. Contact the Royale Service, Inc. at *www.royaleairservice.com* or:

> **Royale Air Service, Inc.**
> *P.O. Box 15184*
> *Duluth, MN 55815*
> *Phone (218) 721-0405 or (877) 359-4753*

Getting Around

Backpackers on a tight time schedule often find it necessary to use intra-island transportation to complete their trip or to meet ferry connections for their return home.

After arriving at Windigo, *Voyageur II* (*www.isleroyaleboats.com*) circumnavigates the Island clockwise and can be used to hop from one section of the park to another. Canoeists and kayakers can also use the ship to skip open stretches of Lake Superior. From Windigo, the vessel stops at McCargoe Cove Campground and Belle Isle Campground and then overnights at Rock Harbor Lodge. The following day, it continues with possible stops at Daisy Farm, Chippewa Harbor Campground, Malone Bay Campground, and Windigo before returning to Grand Portage. You should make arrangements with the captain if you wish to be picked up at locations other than Rock Harbor and Windigo.

Forever/NPS Resorts, which manages Rock Harbor Lodge, also operates a water-taxi service that will drop off backpackers and campers between Rock Harbor and Siskiwit Bay on the south shore and Rock Harbor and McCargoe Cove on the north shore. This avoids the stampede that results when *Ranger III* arrives and 50 to 70 hikers rush down the trail. Once you arrive, inquire at the Rock Harbor store or visitor center for more details or contact in advance (866-644-2003; 906-337-4993 in the summer; *www.isleroyaleresort.com*) and make reservations if arriving during peak season.

A hiker weighs her backpack at Rock Harbor to make sure it's not too heavy.

5   Enjoying The Backcountry

Two kayakers dipped out of Chippewa Harbor at the first light of day and headed west, threading a needle between the rocky shoreline of the Island and the endless expanse of Lake Superior. At the break of dawn, the great lake was smooth and calm, but within an hour the wind had risen and swells appeared. By 9 A.M. pleasant swells became 3-foot waves, some even topped 4 feet and many were cresting.

A 4-foot wave, from the seat of a kayak, towers 2 feet above you. It surges toward the shore like a moving mountain of water, and you lean away from it to climb up one side in the boat and then down the other. In a 4-foot wave, all you see of your partner, if you see anything at all, is a bobbing head. The rest is hidden in the trough.

Too late to turn back, no place to hold up, the kayakers pushed on, knowing that a safe haven awaited them behind a chain of islands that protected Malone Bay. They did not have skirts to cover their cockpits; something they would later agree was a mistake. But still the boats performed well, and when a wave broke over the bow the water would wash harmlessly over the decking and off to the side.

They steadily paddled west, with 100 yards or so between them, until they rounded a head and saw the gap between Isle Royale and Hat Island. On one side, their side, waves were cresting and crashing wildly as a portion of Lake Superior was funneled into the narrow opening. On the other side was calm water and safety. The lead kayaker entered this mad rush of the Lady's fury and was hurled toward the gap, when at the last minute he swung the boat slightly to check on his partner.

The wave hit so hard and so unexpectedly that he never had time to react. It crested over the side and dumped 50 gallons of arctic-like water into the open cockpit. But warmth, or the lack of it, was the last thing on his mind. The water rushed to the front of the boat, buried the bow under the surface, and picked up the stern, rudder and all, out of the lake.

For a split second he found himself waddling in a trough between two waves, with no rudder to turn himself perpendicular to the 4-footer barreling down on him. He braced his knees against the side of the boat, held the two-bladed paddle the way a tightrope walker holds his pole, and threw his weight away from the wave.

Despite being half-full of water and soaking wet gear, the kayak still responded. The boat sluggishly climbed the wave and when it reached the crest, the wave pushed the bow up, the water inside rushed past the kayaker, and the rudder was again where it belonged.

Fueled on adrenaline and fright, he jammed his heel on the foot pedal and made a wide sweeping stroke with the paddle. The kayak turned just in time for the next wave to lift him high on its crest. He shot through the gap like a rock out of a slingshot.

When the boat finally glided to a stop in the still water behind Hat Island, he released his iron grip on the paddle, looked toward the sky, and made the Sign of the Cross, even though he hadn't been in a church in months.

But there was little doubt in his mind that somebody above had an eye on Isle Royale below.

Seeing the Backcountry

There are several ways to venture deep into the park beyond Rock Harbor and Windigo. Backpacking and paddling demand some outdoor experience, good equipment, and a physical desire to travel in a place where motors are not allowed. Camping requires experience and equipment but significantly reduces the need for a strong – and willing – back to carry a pack or boat. But on day hikes, even visitors staying in accommodations at Rock Harbor Lodge can explore remote sections of the Island.

Shoreline Camping

By using intra-park water transportation (see chapter 4) you

Shoreline campers unload their boat for a night at Daisy Farm Campground.

could circle the park and stay at shoreline campgrounds without ever having to haul your gear any farther than from the dock to the first available shelter or campsite. Day hikes with light packs will allow you to easily view much of the park.

Shoreline campers can be well equipped, with little or no weight limit on gear, but still must plan ahead - and carefully. Campgrounds have user's limits that range from one to three days, and water transportation is not a daily service in most areas of the park. Campgrounds that have transportation from either Rock Harbor Lodge or Windigo are McCargoe Cove, Belle Isle, Tooker's Island, Three-Mile, Daisy Farm, Moskey Basin, Chippewa Harbor, and Malone Bay.

Most shoreline campgrounds - those on the coast of Lake Superior - have shelters. The floors are harder to sleep on than the ground, but they are roomier and drier than most tents. Even outdoor purists use them occasionally because they are ideal for sorting and drying out gear after hiking in day-long rain.

Never count on getting a shelter. Always have a tent with you. Shelters are available on a first-come first-serve basis, and at many popular campgrounds they are taken by early afternoon.

Day Hiking
A backpack full of overnight equipment is not necessary to en-

joy a number of hikes from Rock Harbor Lodge. Loops that begin and end at Rock Harbor include the 4.2-mile Albert Stoll Memorial Trail, the 3.8-mile loop to Suzy's Cave and the 10-mile round-trip hike to the top of Mount Franklin along the Tobin Harbor, Mount Franklin Trail and Rock Harbor Trail.

The other way to sneak into the backcountry for a day is to utilize the water bus service that is offered in connection with the cruises on the *MV Sandy*, the concessionaire-operated tour boat. For a reduced fare day hikers can join the tours and then skip the return ride and hike back to Rock Harbor. Twice a week the boat makes a run to Hidden Lake and Lookout Louise and once a week it provides drops-off at Daisy Farm Campground or McCargoe Cove. From Hidden Lake it's a 10.2-mile trek back to Rock Harbor, Daisy Farm is a 7.2-mile hike and McCargoe Cove a 14.4-mile hike. All three walks are for experienced hikers who are in good shape and properly equipped with water, rain gear, food, compass, flashlight, a map and good hiking books.

You can book passage on the *MV Sandy* in advance by contacting Forever/NPS Resorts (866-644-2003; 906-337-4993 in the summer; *www.isleroyaleresort.com*).

Backpacking

Because of the limitations of water transportation, hiking is by far a more popular - and cheaper - way to see the backcountry. The park trails are well marked and easy to follow, with the exception of the rugged Minong Ridge route. You don't have to be a seasoned outdoorsman to hike Isle Royale. Day hikers will find the park ideal for their first weeklong expedition.

But you do have to be in shape and arrive with the proper equipment. For those who are not and who lack the necessary equipment, the Island can be a dangerous place. There are no alpine trails in the park, but there are ridges, and the constant up-and-down trek over them is almost as tiring as hiking in the mountains.

The park has no medical services beyond what rangers can provide with their first-aid kits. A seriously sick or injured person possibly could be stranded for a day or two before help arrives.

Hikers can put together several trail combinations for a weeklong tramp. Most first-time visitors tackle a portion of the Greenstone Ridge Trail, or known simply as "The Greenstone." The trail runs along nearly the entire length of the ridge, from Lookout Louise to Windigo. Backpackers usually skip the first part and hike just the 42 miles from Rock Harbor Lodge to the Island's western end in four or five days. That leaves the final two days of their week's vacation for traveling to and from the park.

The Greenstone Ridge Trail receives the greatest amount of traffic from early July to mid-August. Backpackers who wish to avoid much of that can arrive at Windigo and hike the Feldtmann Ridge, Island Mine, the first leg of the Greenstone, and the Huginnin Cove trails for a five-day circular route. This would include nights at Feldtmann Lake, Siskiwit Bay, Island Mine, and Huginnin Cove scenic campgrounds that are not as busy as those along the Greenstone.

All trails and campgrounds along Rock Harbor are busy during July and August, but by taking a boat to Malone Bay Campground you can escape much of it. From here you could hike Ishpeming Trail, part of the Greenstone to Hatchet Lake, cut across north to the Minong Ridge Trail, and then return to Rock Harbor through the beautiful inland lakes. On this route, nights can be spent at several pleasant campgrounds, including Malone Bay, Todd Harbor, and McCargoe Cove.

For those with backpacking experience who are looking for a more challenging trek, the Minong Ridge Trail is the ideal choice. Much of it lacks boardwalks and bridges and is lightly marked, making it more challenging than any other trail on the Island. The Minong follows a knee-bending, up-and-down pattern along the bare rocky ridge from McCargoe Cove nearly to Windigo.

This trail is a hard, boot-soaking hike, but it rewards backpackers with a good chance to spot wildlife and beautiful views of the Island and Lake Superior. If you plan to go from Rock Harbor Lodge to Windigo, or the other way around, plan on six or seven days. And if you normally cover a mile with a full pack in 30 minutes, plan on some parts of the trail taking you 45 minutes to more than an hour to walk a mile.

If you are unsure where you want to hike, read the rest of this guide and then plan your own route. Keep in mind the following grades used in this book to judge the difficulty of trails:

Easy: An easy-to-follow, relatively level trail that includes bridges and boardwalks through wet areas. An average hiker can cover a mile in 20 or 30 minutes.

Moderate: Most of the trails fall into this category. There is some climbing over ridges, but the path is well marked and boardwalks cross most swamps. Average hikers can plan on covering a mile in

30 to 45-minutes.

Difficult: A poorly marked trail or one that has a considerable amount of climbing. A mile will take 40 minutes to well over an hour on some parts of the Minong Ridge Trail.

Paddling

The third way to see the backcountry, for those who have the equipment and experience, is by paddling. Canoe enthusiasts will claim you work less, see more, and are better able to isolate yourself in the park, something that is very difficult for campers or hikers to do at times.

Most paddlers arrive with a canoe, which is adequate. But remember that park officials strongly recommend that canoeists stay out of the open waters of Lake Superior. Open canoes are too unprotected and unstable for most paddlers to handle the large waves or sudden squalls the lake can kick up.

The alternative to the canoe is a sea touring kayak, and the number of blue-water paddlers (as opposed to white-water kayakers) increases every summer. It's easy to understand why. The decked boat is more stable in rough water and can venture in such areas as Siskiwit Bay or along the south shore. Every year experienced kayakers circumnavigate the Island.

Either way, the price you pay for the easy paddling is portaging your boat and carrying your equipment and food on a second trip. There is no easy way to get around portaging. Some portages are a 75-yard hop, skip, and jump like the Pickerel Cove portage; the one to Lake Richie is a 2.1-mile grunt.

This book divides the park into four areas as far as paddling is concerned. A weeklong canoe trip would mean traveling through two areas with at least one or two portages each day. The four areas are as follows:

The Five Fingers This area at the east end of the park consists of long fiord-like bays, coves, and harbors. It is one of the more beautiful areas to paddle and a personal favorite of many. Although a strong paddler could go from McCargoe Cove to Rock Harbor in a day, you could spend a week exploring each island and cove.

Northern Inland Lakes This area consists of Lake Richie, Lake LeSage, Lake Livermore, Chickenbone Lake, and McCargoe Cove. It is part of a common route where canoeists paddle from Rock Harbor to McCargoe Cove and then cut through the Five Fingers back to Rock Harbor Lodge.

Southern Inland Lakes This area is not as heavily used, and it is here where paddlers can find solitude. The waterways consist of Chippewa Harbor, Lake Whittlesey, Wood Lake, Siskiwit Lake, and Intermediate Lake. The fishing is superb, and anglers will be rewarded with plenty of pike and, possibly, walleye and lake trout. Along with the popular and scenic Malone Bay and Chippewa Harbor campgrounds, there are four canoe campgrounds reached only by paddlers. The Wood Lake Campground is one of the most beautiful and isolated in the park.

Artists on the Island

If there is an artist within you there might be a cabin on Isle Royale for you through the park's Artist-in-Residence Program. Since 1990, the park has hosted four to five artists every summer so they can be stimulated by the remote wilderness that is Isle Royale.

Artists range from painters and writers to poets and musicians and produced a wide range of work including poems, photographs, essays, watercolors, sculptures and songs depicting the beauty and spirit of the Island. Artists are selected by a jury of professional artists and park personnel and spend two to three weeks at the park. They are given the use of a canoe and a rustic cabin. Each artist then conducts a weekly program and donates a piece of art to the park.

A selection of this art was published by the Isle Royale & Keweenaw Parks Association in a hardcover book entitled *The Island Within Us: Isle Royale Artists In Residence*. The coffee table book features full-color reproductions of the art as well as poems and essays by 34 participants of the program in the 1990s.

If you're not that creative consider Isle Royale's Volunteers in Parks Program. Every summer the park hosts volunteers who fill in as an assistant purser on the *Ranger III*, park photographer, on the trail crew, museum technician and many other positions.

For an application to either program contact Isle Royale National Park at (906) 487-7153 or *www.nps.gov/isro*. To order a copy of *The Island Within Us* contact the Isle Royale & Keweenaw Parks Association at (800) 678-6925 or *www.irkpa.org*.

The South Shore It is possible for experienced kayakers with the proper storm gear and enough time to paddle Lake Superior's south shore. The route runs from Rock Harbor through Siskiwit Bay and into the open waters of Lake Superior to Windigo, at the end of Washington Harbor. Kayakers will be in open water for much of the way, but the south shore offers more beaches and coves than its northern counterpart for emergency landings in case of rough conditions. Only experienced kayakers should attempt the north shore from Washington Harbor to McCargoe Cove, because the coastline consists of sharp cliffs with few, if any, places to land.

Before anybody considers paddling the Island, they should be aware of the danger involved in tipping over in Lake Superior. The water, even in the summer, is never more than a few degrees above freezing. Five minutes in Lake Superior and you would be unable to move your fingers. Ten minutes and you would lose control of your legs and arms. Thirty minutes in the lake and you would die of exposure.

The Lady is famous for suddenly turning calm waters into rough seas with high winds or a squall. Canoeists, and especially kayakers considering the south shore, should always plan extra days in case they are forced to sit out stormy weather. Never take a chance in questionable weather just to make the ferry back to the mainland.

Boat Rentals: You can not rent kayaks at either Rock Harbor or Windigo. Canoe rentals are available in Rock Harbor but not Windigo. The park concessionaire, Forever Resorts (866-644-2003; 906-337-4993 in the summer; *www.isleroyaleresort.com*), has 15 to 17-foot aluminum canoes available and offers both a daily and weekly rate.

Cross-Country Travel

The final way of seeing the Island is cross-country travel and camping through the trail-less areas of the park. This adventure is strictly for highly experienced backpackers, because it is a very difficult form of travel. Ponds, marshes, and swamps are scattered throughout Isle Royale, and the Island's north-facing slopes are steep, with some cliffs exceeding 100 feet in height.

Persons interested in cross-country travel must register in advance with park officials and provide a trip itinerary to obtain a camping permit. Kayakers considering the south shore also need the permit, because there are no campgrounds on this section of shoreline and only a limited number of places to land. Keep in mind that certain zones are closed to camping each summer to protect sensitive wildlife habitat; this includes all offshore islands.

Permits and Fees

All park visitors who plan to camp overnight at campgrounds or cross-country sites are required to obtain a camping permit. This permit can be obtained free of charge at the visitor center at Windigo or Rock Harbor when you arrive or on board *Ranger III* on the way to the Island.

The permit allows you to stay in a campground but is not an advance reservation for a site. Occasionally during peak season, you might arrive at a campground with no available sites. If that's the case, park officials say you can do one of several things: move on to the next campground if possible; double up with another party at a site as most contain two or three tent pads; or use the group sites if they are vacant.

Isle Royale National Park also charges a Recreation Fee. The user fee is $4 per person per day or $50 for a season pass and is collected by the ferry or seaplane concessionaires transporting you to the Island. Children 11 years and younger are exempt from the fee.

Backcountry Needs

Prepare for Isle Royale as you would for any wilderness area. Come with the right equipment, but don't arrive with too much. Overweight backpacks is the most common mistake among hikers at Isle Royale, the reason the park has scales at the visitor centers in both Rock Harbor and Windigo. Many backpackers say for a five- or six-day trek, your pack should not exceed one-fourth of your body weight; others, who drill out the center of their toothbrush to reduce weight, say the figure should be closer to one-fifth. What isn't debatable is the fact that if you arrive with a 50-pound pack, you will be miserable on Isle Royale's trails.

Boots: Running shoes won't do in the backcountry. You need good, sturdy, hiking boots that have been worn a few times before you land at Rock Harbor. The new ultralight nylon boots on the market today are an excellent choice for Isle Royale. Footgear should include wool socks while moleskin and bandages should be ready to be applied at the first sign of tenderness.

Tent: Even when it rains, you don't spend much time in your tent, so a lightweight nylon unit that weighs from 6 to 8 pounds is sufficient. It should have a rain fly, bug-proof netting, and a floor whose seams have been waterproofed recently. Also take a sleeping pad to ensure a good sleep every night.

Stove: Opportunities for campfires are very limited and almost nonexistent in the Island's interior campgrounds. Even if you can build them, much of the wood is wet or of poor cook-fire quality. A small, self-contained backpacker stove is a must. You'll be thankful you have it when it rains. White gas is available at the Rock Harbor Lodge and Windigo stores.

Clothes: Come prepared for cool, wet weather - then when the sun breaks out, you won't mind lugging around the extra clothes. Every backpack should have a wool hat and mittens, a heavy jersey or coat, and rain gear (pants and parka). Bring a pair of walking shorts in warm weather.

Insect repellent: Bugs are a part of any wilderness area, and Isle Royale is no exception. From June through mid-August you will be greeted by mosquitoes, black flies, and gnats. Some days are worse than others, but always keep your bug dope within easy reach.

Maps: Every hiking party should have a map and compass and somebody who knows how to use them together. The best map is the *Trails Illustrated Isle Royale National Park* map by National Geographic Maps, which has a scale of 1:62,500. It can be purchased at Windigo, Rock Harbor Lodge, Houghton or from the Isle Royale & Keweenaw Parks Association (800-678-6925; *www.irkpa.org*).

Canoeing equipment: The easiest way to portage a boat is for one person to balance it on his or her shoulders and carry it lengthwise. Use a portage yoke that straps to the sides of the boat. Bring waterproof bags for all gear, especially your sleeping bag, camera, and food. An extra paddle and a repair kit of duct tape and a few tools are also reassuring.

Weather and When to Come

Lake Superior has a great modifying effect. It keeps the winters milder and the summers cooler than those experienced 20 miles away on the mainland. Daytime temperatures range from 60 to 70°F most of the summer and occasionally will exceed 80°F in mid-August. The nights are cool and in early or late summer can easily drop below 40°F.

Thunderstorms and rain showers are common throughout the summer, and dense fog appears frequently in the spring and early

A pair of canoers relax in Rock Harbor before the start of their multi-day paddle across Isle Royale National Park.

summer. The weather can change very quickly, and for that reason some visitors, especially paddlers, pack along a small weather radio. A lighter, alternative is to just schedule a spare day for when the Lady turns rough.

That brings us to the question of when is the best time to visit the park. It all depends on your likes and dislikes. If you can't stand bugs, you will want to arrive mid-August or early September. If you are crazy about wildflowers, mid-June to early July is the best time. Fishermen prefer June, and many backpackers arrive mid- to late September to catch the fall colors or the rutting season of the moose.

The park is officially open from April 16 through Oct. 31, and generally the best weather – sunshine and warm temperatures – occurs from mid-July to mid-August. But that is only a general rule; the Island is full of exceptions from year to year, and the weather is always one of them. It is best to prepare for anything.

An increasing number of paddlers and even backpackers pack along a National Oceanic and Atmospheric Administration (NOAA) weather radio that can be purchased at many outdoor and electronic stores for $25 to $100. With the lightweight receiver you can pick up the NOAA weather reports that are broadcast from Houghton on a frequency of 162.400 Mhz.

Backpackers filter warter in the evening at Three Mile Campground.

The reports include immediate severe storm watches and warnings for the Keweenaw Peninsula and Isle Royale. NOAA also provides seven-day recreational forecasts for Isle Royale, which are updated twice daily and broadcast 5 and 35 minutes past the hour from Memorial Day through Labor Day weekends.

Keep in mind that NOAA broadcasts usually can only be picked up from the southern shore of the Island to the Greenstone Ridge. If paddling the northern shore, you can pick up Canadian weather broadcast from Thunder Bay on 162.475 Mhz.

Even if you're not packing along a receiver, the seven-day recreational forecast can still be heard at the NPS visitors center in Houghton before you head over to the park or in advance from the Marquette National Weather Service at *wwww.crh.noaa.gov/mqt.*

Backcountry Water

Due to the Island's isolation and its lack of deer, there are two things backpackers don't have to worry about when they arrive: the microscopic organism Giardia lamblia and the deer tick that carries Lyme disease. There is, however, the tapeworm. Although no one seems to know the last reported case of a visitor getting tapeworm, park rangers consider all water on Isle Royale to be contaminated with the eggs of the parasite. Only the water from the spigots at Rock Harbor and Windigo is safe to drink without treating.

The tapeworm lives in a cycle that goes from the scat of the wolf to the water and then into the moose when the animal eats aquatic vegetation. The cycle is completed when wolves kill the moose and consume the eggs unknowingly.

It is important to realize that bringing water just to a boil or using iodine or purification tablets will not destroy the eggs. Water must be boiled for at least 2 minutes before the eggs are killed.

An easier alternative is to use a water filter with a screen that will trap particles 0.4 microns or smaller. Any filter on the market today that is suitable for Giardia is more than adequate for tapeworm. Both camp stores usually have filters for sale, but it is cheaper if you buy one before arriving.

In mid-summer, dehydration can be a problem hiking along ridge trails such the Greenstone, Minong and Feldtmann. There are few or no dependable water sources along stretches of these trails and poorly prepared backpackers occasionally run dry. To avoid such situations all hikers should be equipped with enough water bottles to carry 2 quarts per person per day.

Group Camping

A variety of groups, ranging from Boy Scout troops to Audubon societies, plan summer trips at Isle Royale every year. The NPS works closely with groups in advance to ensure their trip is a quality adventure while not adversely affecting the wilderness.

A group is defined as 7 to 10 persons, including leaders. If your party is larger, it will be necessary to split it into two groups, each with independent backcountry itineraries, separate leaders, and different campground stays beginning with the first night. Groups must reserve a Group Camping Permit in advance and stay in designated group sites. The park has 40 such designated sites at 17 campgrounds, including all campgrounds along the Greenstone Ridge Trail.

For group camping reservations and trip planning assistance contact: ***Group Reservations, Isle Royale National Park***

800 E. Lakeshore Dr.
Houghton, MI 49931-1869
(906) 482-0984
Email: ISRO_GroupReserve@nps.gov

What's Available on the Island?

You could almost outfit an expedition at the Rock Harbor store. The small store across from the visitor center has many items, ranging from freeze-dried dinners and trail munches to fishing tackle, pots and day packs. But it's wise not to stock your trip here. The quantities are limited and often run out until the next boat arrives from Houghton while the prices are higher than on the mainland.

The camp store doesn't really cater to newly arrived hikers so much as to those just coming off the trail. Weary backpackers find an incredible selection of sweets to satisfy their junk-food depletion or sugar craving.

Those ending their trek at Rock Harbor have several ways of easing themselves back into civilization. Shower tokens, clean towel, and bar of soap can be purchased at the camp store. After 6 days of freeze-dried turkey tetrazzini, you might want to have dinner at the lodge dining room. Or maybe just a cold beer on the adjacent outdoor deck.

Some backpackers even like to book a room for their final night at Rock Harbor, either at the lodge or in one of the housekeeping units that can be shared by six people and feature small kitchenettes. Reservations are strongly recommended, but visitors can occasionally get last-minute accommodations because of cancellations. For reservations, contact the headquarters of the park concessionaire, located in Kentucky:

Forever Resorts, LLC
P.O. Box 27
Mammoth Cave, KY 42259-0027
(270) 773-2191 or 866-644-2003; www.isleroyaleresort.com

Canoes are also available at Rock Harbor and Windigo for paddling in the local area. The rates are based on a half- or full-day rental and include paddles and life jackets. At Rock Harbor Lodge you can also rent a rowboat and 9.5-horsepower motor. Inquire at the camp stores about rentals.

Low-Impact Camping

The only way the NPS can preserve the Island for future use and still allow the 15,000 to 18,000 visitors to arrive every summer is to practice "low-impact use." The park is fragile, and careless use will disturb its wildlife, delicate plants, and thin layer of soil.

Thus, visitors – hikers and canoeists, especially – must reduce their impact on the land. The Island as we know it will survive only if we are careful in how we treat it. On the back of every backcountry use-permit are these rules:

• Fires are permitted only in metal rings. Use dead and down wood. Do not peel bark or cut live trees.

• Backpackers in interior campgrounds and cross-country campers must use stoves. No wood fires allowed.

Thimbleberries: Tangy Treats Along the Trail

By late August they were exploding along the trail. So many dots of red I didn't have to bend over to pick them. I didn't even stop. I just plucked them from their stems as I hiked along, barely slowing down. Ever few minutes I had a handful. There were still some blueberries around and even

Thimbleberries

an occasional wild raspberry but thimbleberries were the treat on the trail.

That evening in camp I discussed with another backpacker why there were so many out there. We both agreed a lack of bears on Isle Royale definitely had something to do with it. But his theory was that at this time of year the thimbleberry ripens so quickly new ones appear along the trails daily. My theory was that many backpackers, lugging heavy packs, only look three feet in front of their boots. So totally consumed about reaching the next campground, they miss what lies just off the path.

There was no debate that this berry is worth slowing down for.

Thimbleberries are a northern shrub that grows 2 to 5 feet in height and found in thickets in meadows, along the edge of woods, in any natural opening in the forest. Some estimate that thimbleberries could be the most common shrubby ground cover on the Island. Thimbleberry leaves are large, up to 5 inches wide, and resemble maples leaves in shape. Its flowers have five white petals, somewhat triangular in shape, and bloom from late June through July.

The berries begin appearing in early August and are still around in early September, looking like giant red raspberries dangling along the trail. But unlike wild, seedy raspberries, a thimbleberry melts in your mouth and its seeds are so small you hardly notice them. Most of all, it is more tart than sweet and a handful of fully ripened thimbleberries is like a tangy punch in the tastebuds, something every backpacker could use in the middle of a 10-mile day.

When it's raining in early September they are even better. A cold, icy drizzle turns thimbleberries into slightly chilled morsels of tanginess. On a cold, wet day like that a ripe thimbleberry is the only reason most of us would slow down on the trail.

Visitors depart from the Isle Royale Queen IV that sails from Copper Harbor.

• What you pack in, pack out. All trash must be carried out and not burned or buried.

• Pitch tents only in designated sites, as marked in each campground. Do not clear brush away to set up a tent. Groups must camp only in group sites.

• Do not shortcut or start new trails to tent sites in campgrounds.

• Do not shortcut switchbacks or widen trails when they are wet or muddy. Avoid hiking on closed trails and do not start new ones.

• Do not wash or throw wastewater into, or close to any water source, stream, or lake.

• In areas without outhouses, bury feces in a small "cathole," a hole 6 to 8 inches deep and 4 to 6 inches in diameter. When done stir in soil with a stick, cover with two inches of topsoil and disguise with natural material.

• Respect the park's Quiet Hours. If between 10:00 P.M. and 6:00 A.M. the people in adjacent campsites can hear your activities, you are being too loud.

• Do not bring firearms, Frisbees or Fido to Isle Royale. Pets are not allowed in the national park.

• When you break camp, leave no trace.

And please: no radios, boom boxes or CD players while visiting the park. The solitude of nature is too rare and valuable to disturb with man-made music.

Isle Royale
On Foot

Backpackers pause on top of Mount Franklin, a favorite viewing point along the Greenstone Ridge Trail.

6 The Greenstone

❖ *The Greenstone Ridge Trail*

The Island is a maze of footpaths, but it is the longer trails, the ones that reach far into the backcountry, that seem to give hikers their best memories, those "Island moments" that bring some back summer after summer. These are the pathways that lead away from crowded campgrounds and busy shorelines to the solitude that is Isle Royale.

Of the handful of trails that stretch across the park, the Greenstone Ridge Trail is the longest and, without a doubt, the best known. Often referred to as simply "the Greenstone," this route is a Michigan classic, recognized in backpacking circles as one of the premier long-distance routes in the Midwest.

The Greenstone runs along the backbone of the park, stretching from Windigo to Lookout Louise, near the northeast end. In short, it's a walk across the largest island in the largest lake in the world.

That's a notion that many backpackers carry with them from Rock Harbor to Windigo, and when they're standing high on the Greenstone Ridge looking at Lake Superior both to the north and the south it's a notion that reminds them they're in the middle of a watery wilderness.

Greenstone Ridge Trail

Distance: 42.7 miles (Trail plus spurs to campgrounds)
Hiking time: 4-5 days
High point: 1394 feet
Rating: moderate

Although the Greenstone is rated moderate, there is an occasional difficult section with a knee-bending climb. Experienced hikers in good shape can cover the 40-plus miles in 3 days, but the Greenstone can also be a good trail for beginners if they come with light packs and have 4 or 5 days to walk it.

It is debatable which is easier: starting at Rock Harbor or Windigo. The steeper grades are encountered just outside of Windigo, and many hikers prefer to get them over with on the first day. Others like to begin at Rock Harbor and have the rapid walk down Sugar Mountain for the final leg.

For most hikers, transportation arrangements determine where they start. Because the majority of visitors arrive at Rock Harbor, this guide describes the trail from east to west, beginning at Lookout Louise junction.

Ironically one of the most scenic stretches of the Greenstone – from Lookout Louise to Mount Franklin – is the portion most often skipped. Few backpackers take the time to arrange boat transportation from Rock Harbor across Tobin Harbor to Hidden Lake, the start of the Lookout Louise Trail. Most hikers walk either the Tobin Harbor or Rock Harbor Trail and spend their first night at Three Mile Campground. The following day they take the Mount Franklin Trail to the Greenstone (see Chapter 10 and map on page 132).

Rock Harbor

Before jumping on the trail, backpackers have to pass by Rock Harbor Lodge. The visitor center and camp store are immediately in front of you after you disembark from the boat. Backpackers who did not pick up a backcountry use permit from the NPS ranger on *Ranger III* should do so at the visitor center.

The Rock Harbor area – which includes the actual lodge, housekeeping cabins, quarters for concession and NPS workers, and a public campground – can be a busy place with visitors arriving and departing at the same time. Some hikers prefer to pick up their permits and maps and then depart the same day to spend their first night at

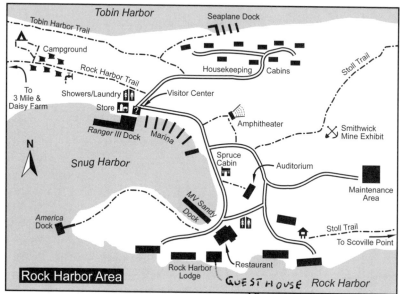

Rock Harbor Area

either Three Mile Campground or Daisy Farm. But most spend their first night in Rock Harbor Campground, which has nine shelters, group and individual campsites, piped-in water, tables, garbage cans, and pit toilets. It is wise to stake out a shelter or a tent site as soon as you arrive: The campground can fill quickly during the height of the summer. There is a one-night limit in the Rock Harbor Campground.

The most important item at Rock Harbor for those new to backpacking is the scale hanging on the backside of the store. Weigh your pack! If it's too heavy now, it's going to be way too heavy once you're on the trail. This is the time to remove excess gear and put it in storage (page 46).

Lookout Louise to Mount Franklin
Distance: 5.1 miles

This is a lightly hiked portion of the Greenstone Ridge Trail because of the need to arrange a drop-off at the Hidden Lake dock. Too bad. The east end of the Greenstone rewards backpackers with some of the best views from the entire trail. The Greenstone begins at the signposted junction with the Lookout Louise Trail. From here the Lookout Louise lies 0.1 mile to the north, Tobin Harbor 0.9 mile to the south, and Windigo 41.0 miles (not including spurs to

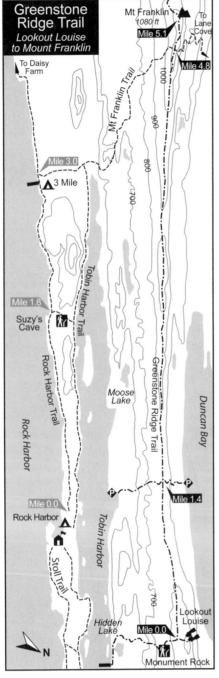

Greenstone Ridge Trail
Lookout Louise to Mount Franklin

Mt Franklin
1080 ft
Mile 5.1

To Lane Cove

Mile 4.8

To Daisy Farm

Mt Franklin Trail

Mile 3.0

3 Mile

Tobin Harbor Trail

Mile 1.8

Suzy's Cave

Rock Harbor Trail

Rock Harbor

Moose Lake

Greenstone Ridge Trail

Duncan Bay

Mile 0.0

Rock Harbor

Tobin Harbor

Mile 1.4

Stoll Trail

Hidden Lake

Mile 0.0

Lookout Louise

Monument Rock

N

campgrounds) at the west end of the Greenstone Trail.

From the junction with the Lookout Louise Trail, the Greenstone quickly departs from the trees and moves to the grassy, open crest of the ridge top. For the next mile the views are wonderful on a clear day. Occasionally you can see Lake Superior on the north side of the Island but more often you're viewing Rock Harbor to the south. Also in this area are ancient copper pits that Indians pounded out 3000 years ago to obtain pure copper. Several, appearing as shallow holes, are near the trail.

The trail continues along the open ridge and quickly becomes one of the most pleasant walks on the Island. Most of the hike is level and easy and passes extensive thimbleberry patches, whose sweet fruit ripens from mid-July to August. Backpackers who hike with their heads to the ground might discover small strawberry patches.

You're still in open terrain when in 1.4 miles from the beginning, the trail arrives at the junction of the Duncan Bay-Tobin Harbor portage. This challenging portage is only 0.8 mile long but climbs 175 feet in an extremely steep fashion.

A day hiker on the Greenstone Ridge Trail east of Mount Franklin.

The ridge top remains exposed for another mile or so with most of the views to the south and then gradually becomes sparsely wooded as you begin climbing gently towards Mount Franklin. Moose signs – prints, droppings, and stripped aspen trees – are plentiful in this area, as are the animals themselves.

The setting stays this way for the remaining 2 miles to the junction with Mount Franklin Trail, reached 4.8 miles from Lookout Louise Trail. To the north is Lane Cove Trail that descends the Greenstone Ridge and in 2.4 miles reaches the pretty little cove and campground. Mount Franklin Trail heads south reaching Three Mile Campground in 2.2 miles to the south.

To the west the Greenstone climbs gently and with 0.3 mile tops off at Mount Franklin (1080 feet), a spot that is more the edge of a steep rocky bluff than a mountaintop. Here, backpackers sit and admire the excellent view of the northeastern end of the park, the outlying islands, and the Canadian shoreline. The small peak was named after Benjamin Franklin.

Mount Franklin to West Chickenbone
Distance: 10 miles

There is little or no water along this stretch of the Greenstone Ridge Trail. If planning to hike from Mount Franklin to West Chickenbone Campground carry 2 quarts of water per person.

From the peak of Mount Franklin, the trail descends quickly into a wooded area and then within a half mile levels out before climbing gently back up to a view of Lake Superior along a grassy ridge top.

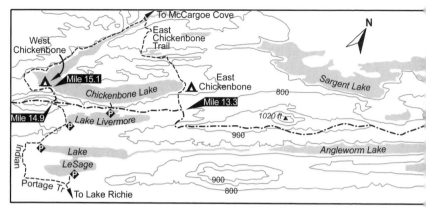

You remain in the open terrain and 1.2 miles from Mount Franklin reach a rocky high point. From this spot you can see both sides of the Island. To the south is Tonkin Bay, West Caribou Island and even Conglomerate Bay, all crowned by Rock Harbor Lighthouse; To the north Canada. This is a very impressive view, missed by those rush to or from Daisy Farm via the shorter and easier Rock Harbor Trail.

The easy hiking and panoramic views remain and 2 miles from Mount Franklin sharp eyes will spot the Mount Ojibway Fire Tower. You reach Mount Ojibway (1136 feet) in another 10 or 15 minutes. The tower is 2.5 miles from Mount Franklin and once was a lookout post for forest fires but now monitors air pollution. You can climb partially up the tower for views on both sides of the Island or simply relax under it for an extended break. This a favorite spot among backpackers and day hikers as it marks the junction with the Mount Ojibway Trail, the first of two trails heading south for Daisy Farm Campground. From here the campground is 1.7 miles away.

The Greenstone departs from the Ojibway Lookout Tower, and

Ben Franklin: Fact or Myth

Mount Franklin was named after Ben Franklin due to what most historians say is a popular myth. While in Paris during the American Revolution it is said the colorful ambassador ran across reports by early French explorers that detailed the existence of copper on Isle Royale. Franklin, already aware of copper's electrical potential from his famous kite experiments, shrewdly made sure Isle Royale was part of the new United States during the negotiations to end the war. The British let it pass even though the island is much closer to Canada than the rest of the U.S.

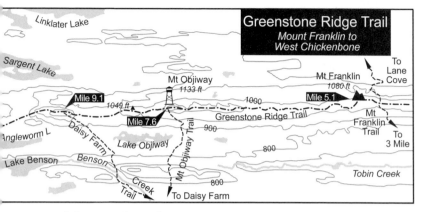

most of the stretch to the next junction follows an open ridgeline. It's an easy and scenic hike, especially in the first 0.5 mile where there are more views of the south shore and Angleworm Lake. In 1.5 miles, the trail reaches the junction of the Daisy Farm Trail, the second trail to Daisy Farm Campground, 1.9 miles to the southeast.

From the junction, the Greenstone goes over several small knolls and then descends toward Angleworm Lake. The first knoll is reached in 0.3 mile and is posted "View Point." From the top of this high rock outcropping you are rewarded with views in both directions, but especially to the north where it's possible to see Canada and Sargent Lake. Eventually the trail levels out and comes within a few hundred yards of the Angleworm Lake to the south. Although thick forest keeps the body of water hidden much of the summer you do get an occasional glimpse of it. There is no maintained side trail to Angleworm Lake, but anglers who want to wet their lines can easily bushwhack to the long, narrow lake to catch northern pike.

Within a mile of passing Angleworm Lake the path gently climbs again, reaches a high point of 934 feet, and then descends to dense forest with scattered bogs. The trail remains in this terrain for a spell before making a gradual ascent to an open crest on the ridge. Here, the birch trees thin out for more than a mile.

The level walk ends near a rock overhang from which you can view the north side of the Island, Pie Island in Ontario, and the east end of Chickenbone Lake. The trail departs from the picturesque spot, descends a little, and then makes a 90° turn. From here it drops quickly off the Greenstone Ridge and uses planking to cross a bog before reaching the junction with the East Chickenbone Trail, which heads 2.1 miles northwest to McCargoe Cove.

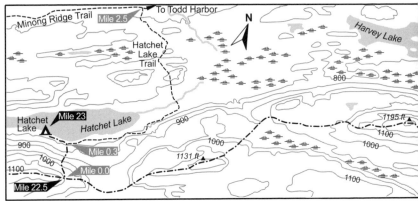

Just 300 feet north of the Greenstone is East Chickenbone Campground, located on a ridge above the east shore of the lake. The campground has individual and group campsites and pit toilets. It is located partially in the trees.

The Greenstone Ridge Trail resumes west from the junction with the East Chickenbone Trail and follows the thin strip of land separating Chickenbone Lake to the north and Lake Livermore to the south. Occasionally through the trees you can catch views of both bodies of water. After 0.6 mile, the trail arrives at the short portage between the two lakes and then dips down to cross a stream. From here it continues for another mile of easy walking until it reaches one of the park's major trail junctions.

This is where the Indian Portage Trail and the Greenstone cross. To the south on the Indian Portage Trail lies Lake Richie (3.4 miles) and Chippewa Harbor (7.7 miles) campgrounds; McCargoe Cove is 2.9 miles to the north. From this point, Hatchet Lake Campground is 7.7 miles west along the Greenstone, and Windigo is 25.8 miles.

The West Chickenbone Campground is 0.2 mile north of the Greenstone Ridge Trail and is a favorite among backpackers. A pretty area situated on the shores of the lake, the campground has individual and group campsites and pit toilets. The lake itself is excellent for pike, yellow perch, and an occasional walleye. Beaver lodges dot the far shore, and moose frequent the waters.

West Chickenbone to Hatchet Lake
Distance: 7.9 miles

Backtrack to the junction of the Indian Portage and Greenstone Ridge trails, a steep climb from West Chickenbone Campground.

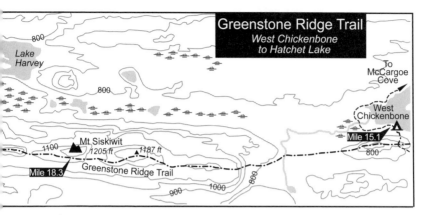

Greenstone Ridge Trail
West Chickenbone
to Hatchet Lake

From the junction the Greenstone climbs up and over a low hill and then levels out for a half mile through a thick forest. After crossing a planked stream, the trail begins its steep climb to Hatchet Lake.

The climb is a backbreaker, especially with a pack on, as you gain 250 feet in less than a half mile. But once you reach the top of the first knoll you are rewarded with perhaps the best view of the inland lakes. Before you to the east are McCargoe Cove, followed by Chickenbone, Livermore, and LeSage lakes. To the south, you can spot Lake Richie, Intermediate Lake, Lake Siskiwit, and Siskiwit Bay.

The fine view is followed by another scenic stretch of the Greenstone Ridge Trail. For the next 3 miles the trail stays high on the ridge and most of the time on the open, rocky crest of it. That includes the first 1.5 miles from the overlook, a stretch open enough for you to view Siskiwit Lake to the south. The trail then gently climbs to a 1160-foot knob, where it's possible to view the north shore of the Island, dips into the trees and begins sidling the grassy southern flank of Mount Siskiwit (1205 feet), 3 miles from the junction to West Chickenbone Campground. The trail never reaches the peak but it would be easy here to drop the packs and scramble to the top.

From Mount Siskiwit the trail descends sharply into the trees for a 0.5 mile and levels out along an open ridge. You eventually resume climbing and reach the high point of 1195 feet where the big slaps of rock and views to the south make it an ideal place for an extended break or lunch. Beyond the knob the path descends in sharp spurts and eventually arrives at a bog, 5.7 miles from the West Chickenbone junction, with a planked stream that has little or no water during dry spells.

In the final 1.5 miles to the Hatchet Lake Trail, you climb over

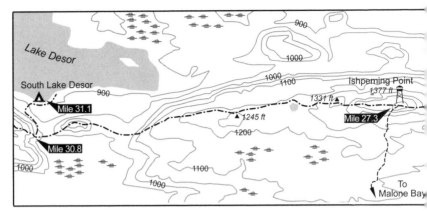

a 1000-foot-plus hill but never break out of the trees, descend and then make the final climb of the day – a short one – to the signposted junction. The Hatchet Lake Trail connects the Greenstone with the Minong Ridge Trail, 2.6 miles to the north. Ishpeming Lookout Tower lies 3.8 miles farther west on the Greenstone, and the junction to West Chickenbone Campground is 7.2 miles to the east.

Hatchet Lake Campground is 0.5 mile from the junction of the Greenstone Ridge Trail. It's reached by first following the spur to Minong Ridge Trail and then heading west along the lake at a posted junction. The individual and groups sites are on a wooded hillside above the lake's south shore and have pit toilets. There is an angler's trail that continues to the west end of the lake. Although there are populations of brook trout, Hatchet Lake is not an angler's hotspot.

Hatchet Lake to South Lake Desor
Distance: 8.1 miles

The Greenstone Ridge Trail departs from the Hatchet Lake junction and climbs for a 0.2 mile to an 1155-foot knob. This is probably the hardest climb of the day for most backpackers because there's no time to warm up and get settled into the rhythm of hiking. Once on top you can catch your breath to a fine view of Siskiwit Lake, Malone Bay, even deep into Siskiwit Bay. The footpath dips up and down between stands of birch and open patches of the ridge, where at times you can see almost the entire lake to the south. Be careful over the rocky areas: You can easily lose the trail.

About 1.5 miles from the junction, the trail climbs steeply and then levels off for a short spell. Keep an eye out for a marked side trail to the right that leads a short distance to rock bluff with in-

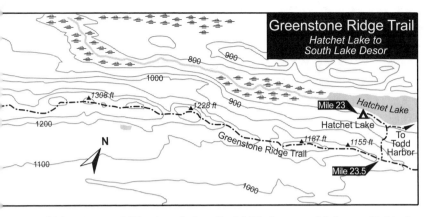

credible views of Hatchet Lake, Todd Harbor, and Mount Siskiwit. The Greenstone Ridge Trail descends briefly again, levels off through birch forests, and then sharply climbs to more scenic views.

From here the trail winds through open clearings for half mile before it makes another noticeable descent. The trail levels off for a short distance and begins its final half-mile climb to Ishpeming Point (1377 feet), the second highest point on Isle Royale.

The climb is an easy one and suddenly you pop out of the woods at the Ishpeming Point Tower with no forewarning. There is a lookout tower, one of the lowest ones I've ever come across. Now used for research by the park staff, the tower was built when Ishpeming Point was bald but now the surrounding trees are taller than the structure so there is no view whatsoever. If it's raining, however, this is a wonderful spot to have lunch, as its platform will keep you dry.

Ishpeming Point is also the junction to Malone Bay with Ishpeming Trail departing south and reaching the campground in 7 miles. The tower is almost halfway between Lake Desor (3.8 miles) and Hatchet Lake Campground (4.3 miles) along the Greenstone.

The next segment to Lake Desor is completely different from the trek from Hatchet Lake. The walk to Lake Desor seems shorter and has less up-and-down hiking but provides few views except for the trees next to the path. The trail departs west from the lookout tower and immediately descends and levels out. For the next 2 miles you follow the rolling crest of the ridge without enduring any great climbs. Halfway through this stretch you break out to a small pond surrounded by an open bog, a good place to look for wildlife.

The trail then climbs steeply and tops off at 1245 feet where it follows an open ridge briefly to a rocky knob. From here you're fi-

Father and daughter follow the Greenstone Ridge Trail to Windigo.

nally rewarded with a view: Lake Desor to the west with the Minong Ridge behind it. If you're not in a hurry to set up camp you can climb the outcropping to admire the best view of the day.

If you are in a hurry, the spur to the campground is still a mile down the trail. From the knob the trail descends steadily but not sharply for 0.7 mile, bottoming out in a low-lying woods. It levels out and shortly reaches the junction of the trail to South Lake Desor Campground. The campground is 0.3 mile from the junction of the Greenstone Ridge Trail; Island Mine Campground is 5.2 miles farther west along the Greenstone.

Although situated above the shoreline and not on it, the South Lake Desor Campground is a favorite among backpackers. The individual and group campsites are located in a stand of birch and often there is a little breeze to keep the bugs at bay. Near the first group site is a small sandy cove where campers occasionally take a dip or in the evening watch the sun set while listening to the resident loons. Like Desor supposedly has brook trout in it, but it is not heavily fished.

South Lake Desor to Windigo
Distance: 11.6 miles

This is a long day so start early! For many backpackers, however, this is also their final day so their packs are light and their legs are strong. Just the vision of junk food or a hot shower in Windigo is usually enough to propel them down the trail.

The Greenstone Ridge Trail departs from the junction of the campground trail and immediately makes a steep ascent to the ridge.

It climbs over a hump, where there are views of Lake Desor, drops slightly, and then makes another ascent to an 1105-foot high point on the ridge. Here the trail swings near the edge of the ridge and 1.5 miles from the Lake Desor junction a side trail leads to a rocky clearing in the trees.

From this spot you can see the Canadian shoreline to the north and flat-topped Pie Island in Lake Superior. Enjoy the sun and the breaks in the foliage; these are the last significant views for the remainder of the trail.

The Greenstone steeply climbs to the high point of 1319 feet, descends briefly to a marshy area crossed by planking and then makes its final and steepest climb to the top of Mount Desor (1394 feet), the highest point on the Island. Arriving at the summit is a disappointment, because it is covered with sugar-maple trees and offers no views. It's simply a wide spot in the trail with a couple boulder in the middle of it. Without any signposts, some hikers go right by without ever realizing they have just climbed to the park's loftiest perch.

From the mountain, the trail descends gradually for more than a mile, where it levels out and crosses a

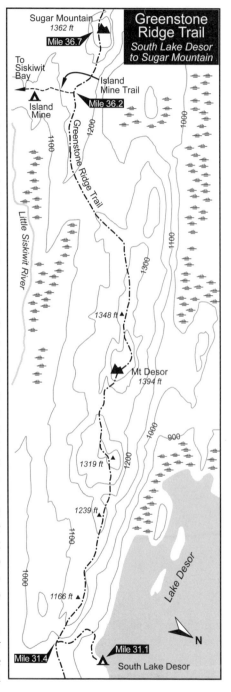

Greenstone
Ridge Trail
*South Lake Desor
to Sugar Mountain*

Sugar Mountain
1362 ft
Mile 36.7

To Siskiwit Bay

Island Mine Trail
Mile 36.2

Island Mine

Greenstone Ridge Trail

Little Siskiwit River

1348 ft

Mt Desor
1394 ft

1319 ft

1239 ft

1166 ft

Mile 31.4

Mile 31.1

Lake Desor

N

South Lake Desor

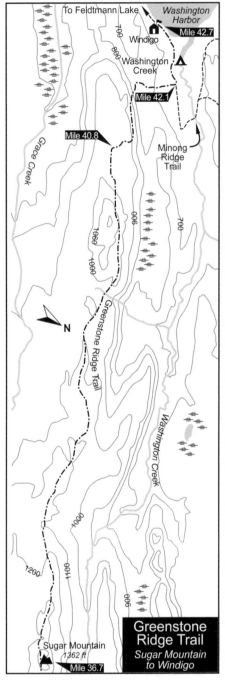

Greenstone Ridge Trail

Sugar Mountain to Windigo

swamp. Most of the trail has been planked so backpackers don't have to wander through knee-deep mud.

Eventually, the footpath makes a long climb up the ridge and then levels out for 0.3 mile before arriving at the junction with the Island Mine Trail. To the south, along this side trail, are Island Mine Campground (0.4 mile) and Siskiwit Bay Campground (4.8 miles). Lake Desor Campground lies 5.1 miles to the east at this point, and Washington Creek Campground is 6.2 miles to the west.

The Island Mine Campground is in a sugar-maple forest and provides individual and group campsites and pit toilets. Water is available from a nearby stream that's cool and clear. This is the only campground not bordering an inland lake, cove, or Lake Superior, but from late September to mid-October, when the trees show off their brilliant fail colors, Island Mine is a great place to pitch a tent.

By this time, many hikers prefer to push on to Windigo. The Greenstone Ridge Trail departs from the junction with the Island Mine Trail and gradually climbs the remaining 0.5 mile to the top of Sugar Mountain (1362 feet), the third highest point on the

An Oilcan at the End of the Trail

Because I was solo hiking at Isle Royale for 12 days – far too many to carry all my food – I arranged to have some supplies shipped to Windigo, the halfway point of my trek.

Along with freeze-dried dinners, extra fuel, batteries and another paperback, I placed a can of Fosters beer in the box. Not just a regular can but the 25-ouncer they call "the Oilcan." When I emerged from the Minong Ridge Trail, I picked up the box and placed the can in Lake Superior. Then after dinner that evening I sat down in my campsite to enjoy an ice cold beer in the middle of the wilderness.

I was on the verge of popping the tab when I noticed somebody was watching me; a 30-year-old backpacker who looked liked he had spent too many days eating gorp on the trail.

"I'll give you $5 for that," he said eyeing my Fosters.

"No way, it cost me $2.50 at home."

"Okay, I'll give you $7 for that beer."

None of this shocked me.

The lesson you learn backpacking across Isle Royale is that you need very little to survive, that everything required to live for a week you can carry on your back. But what motivates many of us to reach the end of the trail is the thought of finally indulging in some of the things we don't need. This famine-to-feast transition is best seen at the small store in Windigo. On almost any afternoon there'll be a dozen backpackers outside consuming entire packages or Oreo cookies or a two-pound bag of Cool Ranch Doritos while washing them down with two or three Cokes. You can enjoy a lot of luxuries at Windigo - chewy Chips-Ahoy! cookies, a hot shower, a flush toilet, even load of clean laundry - but you can't get everything some of us crave. A cold can of beer is one of them.

Not wanting to appear selfish with my Fosters, I pushed the price up in hopes of discouraging this deprived backpacker.

"Tell you what, for $10 I'll split this can with you."

I thought that was it, that he was on the verge of leaving when I made a big mistake. I popped the top. That initial "phsssst" followed by dark lager foam spreading across the top of the can was too much for him.

"Okay," he said pulling out a couple of crinkled bills from his pocket. "But you can't tell my buddies in the next campsite I had a beer without them."

Island, although you might not realize it. There's no sign, view, or even a break in the trees to tip hikers off that they have reached the peak. The only indication is you begin descending for the first time since the junction.

The mountain is named after the sugar-maple trees that cover it and the forest much of the way to Windigo. As late as the 1870s, Indians arrived at Sugar Mountain to tap the trees for their sweet sap.

From Sugar Mountain, you descend gradually for a half mile and then level out and at 1.5 miles from the Island Mine junction cross the largest stream of the day via a series of small boulders. In late summer this stream can be dry. The trail remains level and in another 1.5 miles follows a narrow ridgeline of the Greenstone, where you'll easily be able to look down into the forest on both sides.

The trail resumes its gentle downhill trend but 5 miles from the Island Mine junction makes a 90° swing to the north, followed by a rapid descent off the Greenstone Ridge, dropping more than 300 feet in less than a mile. For those who have been following this ridge for the past five days, this can be a rather sentimental moment. Others are only happy to make the descent and head for Windigo. Once off the ridge, you quickly arrive at the Minong Ridge Trail. To the west on the trail are Washington Creek Campground (0.3 mile) and the Windigo Ranger Station (0.6 mile). From this point, Island Mine Campground is 6.3 miles via the Greenstone Ridge Trail.

At Washington Creek Campground, it's wise to stake out a shelter before continuing on. The campground has 10 shelters along the creek, toilets, tables, and piped-in water, along with individual and group campsites. The creek is known for its fine brook trout fishing and an angler can occasionally catch a pike. There is usually a camp moose – if not a couple – visiting the stream at dusk.

Another 0.3 mile west is Windigo, where there are public showers, a small laundry facility and flush toilets along with a small store, a visitor center, and a major boat dock. The visitors center was opened in 1999 and is a short climb from the Windigo dock. Inside are displays and exhibits of the park, a small library and sales counter that sells park publications and issues backcountry permits. From the center a short trail leads to the amphitheater and store.

A short distance out in the harbor is Beaver Island, where at its west end is a campground with three shelters and a dock. The island and its shelters are a popular stop for boaters.

From Windigo, you can catch a boat back to Grand Portage or to Rock Harbor Lodge (see page 49).

7   The Long Trails

❖ *Minong Ridge Trail*
❖ *Feldtmann Ridge and Island Mine Trails*
❖ *Rock Harbor and Lake Richie Trails*

The Greenstone Ridge Trail is the best known footpath on the Island but hardly the only one. Within the park, several other long-distance trails can be combined for am extended tramp in the woods.

Experienced backpackers who enjoy a little challenge in their hiking would do well to skip the Greenstone and undertake the Minong Ridge Trail, a hike of more than 30 miles. The trail has been intentionally kept in a rugged and undeveloped state to serve as a more challenging alternative to the easier hiking found on the Greenstone. On the Minong there is a lack of boardwalks, bridges and posted mileage signs found on most other trails in the park. The Minong rewards you with fewer backpackers, more wildlife encounters and outstanding views of the Island's north shore.

If the desire to seek out solitude excites you but not the ruggedness of the Minong Ridge, there's the Feldtmann Ridge and Island Mine trails. This 23.5-mile loop is well bridged, marked, and relatively moderate in difficulty but doesn't experience the use that the Greenstone does. Highlights of the trip would include a sunset stroll along beautiful Rainbow Cove, the panoramic view from the tower on Feldtmann Ridge, and Siskiwit Bay Campground – a pleasant spot to spend a night.

The third long-distance route on Isle Royale is the Rock Harbor Trail, a mild-to-moderate hike that runs from Rock Harbor Lodge along the shoreline to Moskey Basin, 11.0 miles away. The trail can be combined with the 1.9-mile Lake Richie Trail and portions of the Indian Portage and Greenstone Ridge Trail for a circular 5-day hike from Rock Harbor Lodge through the northern inland lakes.

❖   ❖   ❖   ❖

MINONG RIDGE TRAIL

Distance: 31.4 miles (Trail plus spurs to campgrounds)
Hiking time: 4-5 days
High point: 1047 feet
Rating: Difficult

Occasionally called "Michigan's toughest trail," the Minong Ridge Trail was cut in 1966 as a "fire manway," a route fire fighters could use to access the isolated northern half of the Island. Almost from the beginning backpackers began following the route and eventually the park decided to manage it as a primitive trail with as few markers, bridges and boardwalks as possible.

Part of the challenge of Minong Ridge is the amount of time needed to hike it. The trail itself is a three to four-day walk from McCargoe Cove Campground to Windigo. But most backpackers also need another two days to reach McCargoe Cove from Rock Harbor. Carrying six days worth of food and fuel makes for a heavy backpack on a trail where you want to be as light as possible.

Due to the lack of bridges and planking, you inevitably get your boots soaked when hiking the Minong and occasionally have to retrace your steps after losing the path. Moose are heavily active in the area, and their paths are occasionally mistaken for the trail.

But what makes the Minong so demanding is the constant up-and-down hiking over the bare-rock ridge. The hard surface quickly tires the feet and results in aching arches at night; the uneven route – stepping from rock to rock – is hard on the ankles. Hikers planning to undertake the trail should arrive in good walking shape, plan on taking 45 minutes to an hour to cover a mile, and expect to spend the nights massaging their feet.

The payoff is frequent sightings of wildlife - especially moose - great views of the north shore and Canada from on top of the ridge, and few encounters with other hikers. Nights can be spent in three of the park's nicest shoreline campgrounds; McCargoe Cove, Todd Harbor, and Little Todd Harbor.

The Minong Ridge is best hiked from east to west, leaving the

Two campers at Todd Harbor enjoy the view of Lake Superior.

long portion from Lake Desor to Windigo for the end. Plan on at least 4 hiking days to go from McCargoe Cove to Windigo and no less than 6 to tramp from Rock Harbor Lodge to Windigo via the Minong Ridge, a trek of more than 48 miles. One way around this is to utilize the *Voyageur II* or the lodge concessionaire water taxi to be dropped off at McCargoe Cove.

If you're following the trail from mid-July to mid-August, when the summer temperatures usually peak on the Island, start the day early and carry 2 quarts of water per person. It can get hot on the open ridge and water can be hard to find at times, particularly between Little Todd Harbor and North Lake Desor.

The other thing that makes the Minong Ridge Trail unique is the use of cairns to mark the route. No other trail in Michigan uses cairns so extensively. Along many open stretches you are simply hiking from cairn to cairn and at times it's easy to miss the next one. If you become temporarily turned around on the ridge, pause and search for a cairn or backtrack to the last one you passed and start again. Because the Minong Ridge is not nearly as heavily traveled as the Greenstone, where the route dips from a rocky ridge into the woods it is not always an easy-to-distinguish path. Be prepared to search for the trail from time to time on the Minong Ridge.

Copper Mining on the Minong Ridge

Of all the copper mining that took place on Isle Royale, Minong Ridge near McCargoe Cove was the site of the most intense activity and today is the best place on the Island to see the artifacts and ruins that miners left behind.

It's estimated that Indians began mining along the ridge more than 4,500 years ago. Using rounded, hand-held stones gathered on the beaches, Indians would pound at veins visible on the surface to extract the raw copper from the Minong Ridge. The resulting prehistoric pits are among the oldest known mines in North America.

It was the discovery of those ancients pits that lead prospectors in 1872 to stake out Minong Mine, Isle Royale's largest and most productive. By 1875 the mining company was employing 50 men who lived in Cove. Located at the south end of McCargoe Cove, the small settlement had a post office and at one time was the seat of government for a separate township within what was then Isle Royale County. Miners also had a stamp mill, powered by a dam across Chickenbone Creek, and a railroad that ran from a dock on McCargoe Cove to the mine site.

Miners sank two shafts along the ridge, one more than 300 feet, but most of the work was done in open pits. In 1876, the mine recovered 30 tons of copper and from 1875 to 1885 it removed 249 tons, including a 6,000-pound nugget. By 1879, however, the deposits were already dwindling and all mining worked ceased by 1885.

A side trip to the mine site is a round-trip walk of 3 miles from McCargoe Cove. Begin on the Minong Ridge Trail and within 0.8 mile you arrive a signpost that announces "Todd Harbor 6.6 Miles" on it. A spur here veers off to the left and within a quarter mile the trails begins climbing over piles of loose rock, the tailings leftover from the mining era. Be careful when hiking across the slopes of tailings. A sharp eye will also spot metal work, mostly rail lines and the wheels from ore carts.

In a half mile from the junction you'll pass one of the open pits, now appearing as a pond, and eventually will arrive at the shafts. Again extreme caution must be used if entering the old shafts. If your itinerary doesn't include McCargoe Cove, keep in mind that the *MV Sandy* includes a hike to the mine during its weekly North Side Cruise, an 8 to 9-hour, range-accompanied boat tour from Rock Harbor Lodge.

McCargoe Cove to Todd Harbor
Distance: 6.6 miles

No matter how you arrive at McCargoe Cove, by foot, paddle, or ferry plan on spending a night at this beautiful campground. The site has 6 shelters, individual and group campsites, toilets, and tables. There is also a dock where a pleasant evening can be spent watching beaver, waterfowl, or moose feeding across the cove.

A trail begins near Cabin No. Six in the campground and climbs gently for 0.8 mile, where it levels out briefly and arrives at the first of two junctions with side trails to Minong Mine.

This side trail runs parallel with the Minong Ridge for less than a 0.5 mile until it reaches the site of the Minong Mine, Isle Royale's largest copper mine, operated 1874-1883. The area is marked by large piles of rock tailings, rails, and ore cars from the small railroad that hauled rock from several shafts to the cove. Along the way, you can spot many small pit mines where prehistoric Indians pounded out pure copper.

The Minong Ridge Trail departs the junction to Minong Mine and ascends steeply. At one point, you will pass an unmarked second junction to the Minong Mine and then 1.5 miles from the campground break out at the rocky crest of Minong Ridge and the first of many great views of the north shore of Isle Royale and Canada. Starting here, hikers must be careful to keep an eye out for rock cairns. It is very easy to wander off in the wrong direction and frustrating when you have to backtrack to locate the last marker.

You will also begin the rugged up-and-down trek along the Minong Ridge, following the crest of the ridge but dipping every so often into a stand of trees. Your feet will feel every loose rock you stumble over, making most backpackers ponder whether they remembered to pack Moleskin.

Within a mile after reaching the open ridge, Otter Lake unexpectedly appears to the north as a deep blue gem in a green setting. Sharp eyes will even spot the east end of Todd Harbor from this spot. You continue along the ridge and in the next 0.5 mile will break out to two more views of the lake; the second time is where you're standing at the edge of a rocky cliff with Otter Lake straight below you.

Once past the lake the trail enters the woods and stays in the forest the remaining 2.0 miles to Todd Harbor. Along the way, it continues to drop and climb as it passes through swamps, but the hike is considerably easier than the beginning on the rocky ridge top. Pause

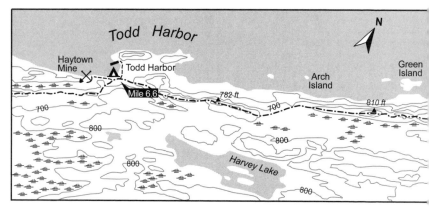

and search each marsh carefully, moose often feed there.

Within 1.5 miles of the campground you cross a small stream where drinking water is easily accessible. The trail continues in the woods then finally, 0.5 mile from Todd Harbor, the trail swings toward the lakeshore, crosses a stream, and works its way down to the shore of the harbor. At times you can feel the cool lake breeze through the trees before you arrive at the campground.

Todd Harbor is a favorite among backpackers, because the protected water is usually calm and peaceful and the view across the bay is stunning during sunsets. The campground has one shelter, group and individual campsites, pit toilets, a fire ring, and a dock. If a northerly wind is blowing, Todd Harbor will be bug-free.

From near the fire ring a trail heads 0.2 mile west to the Haytown Mine. This mine held some of the richest copper deposits on the Island but its isolated location and lack of protection from strong northerly winds made the operation unprofitable. The mine operated from 1847 to 1853. Today all that remains is a shaft that has been fenced off and a pile of rock tailings.

Todd Harbor to Little Todd Harbor

Distance: 6.7 miles (includes spur to campground)

From Todd Harbor the trail climbs briefly and then, in a surprisingly level walk, covers the first 1.4 miles in birch forest. It dips only twice to cross streams and then returns to its pleasant stroll – unlike the grunt from McCargoe Cove. A quarter mile from the footbridge over the second stream the trail reaches the junction of the side trail to Hatchet Lake and the Greenstone Ridge. The Hatchet Lake Trail swings south to pass the junction to the lakeshore campground

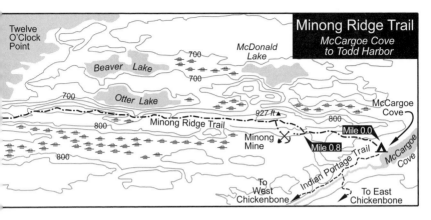

Minong Ridge Trail
McCargoe Cove to Todd Harbor

(2.3 miles) and eventually to reach the Greenstone Ridge Trail (2.6 miles). From the Hatchet Lake northern trailhead, Little Todd Harbor is another 5.3 miles along the Minong Ridge Trail.

You depart west for Little Todd Harbor and for the next 0.5 mile continue to enjoy an easy walk through the woods and then make an ascent back to the ridge top. The trail follows the up and down crest of the ridge for the next 3 miles. You never completely break out of the trees along this segment but within a mile begin treading along a narrow spine of rock where both sides of the Minong Ridge drop steeply below you. You can get a glimpse or two through the trees here of the north shore of the Island and Lake Superior.

The next 2 miles continues to follow the jagged contour of the Minong Ridge. You never climb or descend very far but it seems like the trail is always either going up or down. This can sap your energy and make for a tiring end to a long day on the trail. Roughly 4 miles from the junction with the Hatchet Lake Trail, the Minong Ridge Trail skirts a large grassy marsh to the south. The first thing you instinctively look for is a moose. Then you become aware of the towering bluff that borders the other side of the marsh. It's the Greenstone Ridge, looking much more imposing at this point than the Minong.

The trail returns to the forest and in a half mile swings to the north to descend to a stream. There's no footbridge at this unnamed stream, just a series of logs to tip toe over. You climb the bank on the other side and then begin a rapid descent. The trail bottoms out to cross a small stream and then arrives at the junction with the side trail to Little Todd Harbor.

The trail to the Little Todd Harbor Campground is a gradual 0.6-

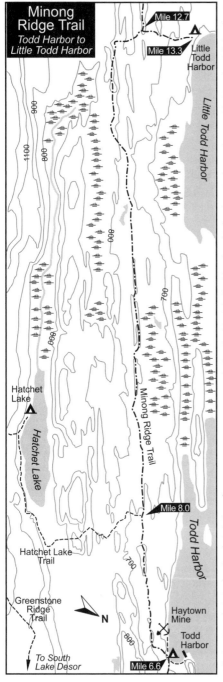

Minong
Ridge Trail
*Todd Harbor to
Little Todd Harbor*

Mile 12.7

Mile 13.3 Little
Todd
Harbor

Little Todd Harbor

900

1100 800

800

700

Hatchet
Lake

Hatchet Lake

Minong Ridge Trail

Mile 8.0

800

Todd Harbor

Hatchet Lake
Trail

700

Greenstone
Ridge
Trail N

Haytown
Mine

Todd
Harbor

800

To South
Lake Desor Mile 6.6

mile descent to the shoreline, with two steep drops to cross a pair of bogs. There are no shelters at Little Todd Harbor and the individual sites, arranged in two clusters, lack privacy if more than two parties are spending the night. Still, after a tiring day on the Minong Ridge, this is a pleasant place to rest those aching muscles. Little Todd Harbor is not quite the island-studded setting that you enjoyed at Todd Harbor but it lends itself to a feeling that you are in a much more remote spot. The individual campsites are near the shoreline, where at night you can fall asleep to the lapping water of Lake Superior. Each site has a pit toilet and a fire ring, but there is no group camping.

Little Todd Harbor to North Lake Desor

Distance: 5.7 miles (includes spurs to campgrounds)

The section between Little Todd Harbor and the junction of the trail to Lake Desor follows bare ridge most of the way and is the hardest part of the trail. Even a hiker in good walking shape will need 4-6 hours to cover this stretch. If the day promises to be hot and sunny, make sure you pack along sufficient drinking water, 2 quarts per person.

The trail departs from the junction of the trail to Little Todd Harbor and immediately climbs out of the birch and aspen forest to the rocky crest of the ridge. At the top, you have gained enough elevation for an unobstructed view of the Greenstone Ridge to the south, Lake Superior to the north, or more of the ridge straight ahead.

The trail continues to follow the open ridge but occasionally dips in and out of the forest in a pattern that will become all too familiar by the end of the day. Again, a word of caution for hikers: Keep your eye out for the trail markers - rock cairns, orange arrows, or orange tags imbedded in the sides of trees.

Within a 0.5 mile of reaching the open crest of the ridge you arrive at another panoramic view; on the horizon is Lake Superior and the Canadian shoreline, straight below are the islets called Gull Rocks. You continue with that up-and-down pace and 2 miles from the junction arrive at the best view of the day. While standing on the edge of a steep rocky cliff that is the Minong Ridge here you can see all the way back to Todd Harbor to the east.

The trail continues to follow the ridge and 2.5 miles from the junction to Little Todd Harbor begins to skirt the bluffs above an unnamed lake. The lake remains in view off and on for the next 0.5 mile and then the trail finally makes a significant descent into the forest, a moment of relief for the soles and ankles of your feet.

Alone on the Minong Ridge

Once during a solo trip in early September, I spent three days alone on the Minong Ridge Trail. I didn't encounter anybody from the time I left Todd Harbor Campground until I reached Windigo. Three days when I never heard a human voice except when I accidentally dropped my pot of macaroni and cheese one night.

It's an experienced I've had before – for much longer periods of time even – but one that no matter how short never ceases to amaze me. For 70 hours there were no cars, no radios, no Facebook, no neon lights, no requests, no conversations. No other people.

But it wasn't quiet. Once you stop listening to the noise we make, you become acutely aware of the natural sounds that fills the woods. I spent three days listening to the wind, and loons laugh, to insects that clicked non-stop in the evening and a squirrel who chattered at me every time I sat down to eat at North Lake Desor Campground.

I spent 14 days on Isle Royale during that trip and in this remote corner of Lake Superior managed to be alone for three of them. In this crowded world of ours, that might be the best I can hope for.

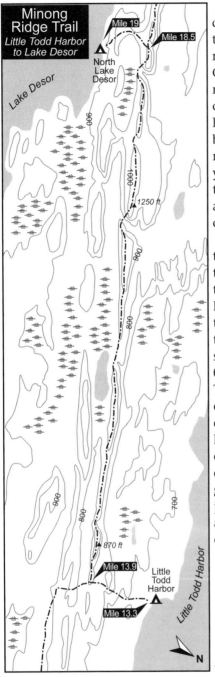

Minong Ridge Trail
Little Todd Harbor to Lake Desor

Mile 19
Mile 18.5
North Lake Desor
Lake Desor
900
1000
1250 ft
900
800
800
900
700
870 ft
Mile 13.9
Little Todd Harbor
Mile 13.3
N

The relief is short lived because the trail climbs back to the open ridge to begin the final 2 miles to North Lake Desor Campground. This is the most rugged stretch of the day because twice you are faced with long climbs out of the woods back to the top of Minong's rocky backbone. But each time you top off there are views of the north shore of the Island and Canada to enjoy while catching your breath.

Eventually you descend off the rocky crest and just inside the trees arrive at the signpost that marks the side trail to North Lake Desor Campground. At the end of a long day, the spur to the campground for many seems like a lot longer than the 0.5 mile indicated on the map. The trail winds through the forest as it gently descends to the campground. North Lake Desor has a pit toilet and individual campsites but no group site or, for that matter, much level ground. Along the shoreline just east of the campground is a small sandy cove ideal for a cool dip in the lake.

North Lake Desor to Washington Creek

Distance: 12.6 miles (includes spurs to campgrounds)

Although this section is not as difficult as the previous seg-

Backpackers follow the Minong Ridge Trail near North Lake Desor.

ments along the Minong Ridge, it is the longest one and requires a full day with a backpack on. Despite a natural eagerness to reach Windigo, take your time, and keep your eye on the trail to pick up the occasional rock cairns. This stretch can get confusing when it crosses a couple of beaver ponds.

The trail departs from the junction of the trail to North Lake Desor Campground and immediately climbs and follows the ridge for 0.5 mile. You then dip back into the forest and a mile from the junction to North Lake Desor begin a steep climb. The reward at the top is a grand view of Lake Desor over your shoulder.

You remain on the rocky ridge for another 0.5 mile and then de-

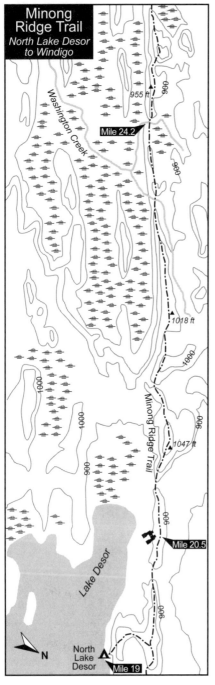

scend into a beautiful birch forest. The trail stays in the forest for 2 miles then climbs to the ridge covered by thimbleberry bushes. The break in the trees is brief as the trail descends back into a low-lying forest with a marshy stream that is crossed on a series of logs.

After crossing the stream you make a steep climb to break out at a small clearing on Minong Ridge. This is the first of four openings you climb to in the next 2 miles that for the most part is an up-and-down walk in the woods. After the third clearing, the trail descends sharply and bottoms out in a marshy area that is crossed by an extremely long stretch of planking.

From the planking, you're faced with the fourth and longest climb that tops off at a stretch of rocky crest. You descend to a small pond that is crossed via a beaver dam, climb again and, 9 miles from the junction to North Lake Desor, descend to a second beaver pond. This one is larger, meaning the beaver dam you use to cross it is longer and more challenging. Be careful!

You climb again once across with the steep ascent ending at a high rocky point known as Minong Trail Overlook, a popular day hike destination from Windigo. The view is not as panoramic as others you have witnessed along the Minong Ridge Trail but you can spot parts of Canada, Pie Island, and Washington Harbor to the southwest. You are now 3 miles from Washington Creek Campground.

The trail descends from the overlook towards Washington Creek Basin and crosses a branch of the creek. This area is popular with moose so keep a sharp eye out for them. The trail swings west and resumes climbing and 1.8 miles from the Minong Overlook reaches the marked junction of East Huginnin Cove Trail. The scenic cove and campground (see page 114) lie 3.3 miles to the north, while Washington Creek Campground is 1.5 miles west and North Lake Desor Campground is 11.1 miles east. Just 0.3 mile up East Huginnin Cove Trail are the posted ruins of the Wendigo Mines.

From the junction, you descend the last bit of the Minong Ridge for 0.6 mile, bottoming out at the southern trailhead of the West Huginnin Cove Trail. From this junction, the cove is 3.1 miles to the north. Just to the south the Minong Ridge Trail descends and crosses Washington Creek. At the bridge there is a hydrologic benchmark station. Stream measurements and water samples are taken almost

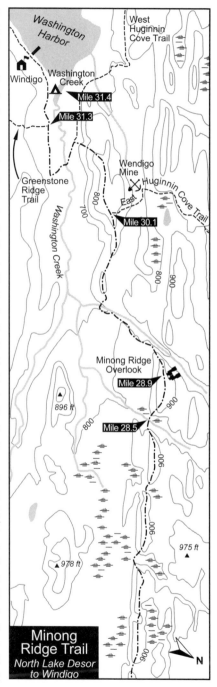

daily here, and scientists use the data from this isolated station as a comparison with those from urban areas to determine the effect of human activity on our water supply.

On the south side, the trail climbs out of the creek basin and in 0.6 mile arrives at the west end of the Minong Ridge Trail where it merges into the Greenstone Ridge Trail. To the west Washington Creek Campground, with piped water, 10 shelters, and individual and group sites, is only 0.3 mile away, while the ranger station and ferry dock at Windigo is 0.6 mile. East on the Greenstone Ridge Trail, the junction to Island Mine Campground is 5.9 miles.

❖   ❖   ❖   ❖

FELDTMANN RIDGE AND ISLAND MINE TRAILS

Distance: 23.6 miles
Hiking time: 3 days
High point: 1200 feet
Rating: Moderate

The Feldtmann Ridge-Island Mine circuit is a pleasant walk that takes you into the southwest part of the park and provides a glimpse into the extensive swamp along Big Siskiwit River – perhaps the most desolate corner of Isle Royale.

The only steep climbs in the hike are over the Feldtmann and Greenstone ridges; the rest of the trek tends to be relatively level. Many backpackers like to hike to Feldtmann Lake Campground first, making the final day a downhill walk along the Greenstone Ridge to Windigo. One difficult part of the trail is the 10.3-mile hike from Feldtmann Lake Campground to Siskiwit Bay. The trek, which involves traversing the Feldtmann Ridge, can be long and tiring.

The first leg of the trail, from Windigo to the junction of the trail to Feldtmann Campground (8.5 miles), is also known as the Feldtmann Lake Trail. Parts of this trail were re-routed in the early 1990s and the trek now includes an overlook 2 miles from Windigo, making it a popular choice for day hikers.

Windigo to Feldtmann Lake Campground
Distance: 8.5 miles

Start in front of the Windigo ferry dock and follow the road west to the trailhead. Within a quarter mile you pass a posted junction with the Windigo Nature Trail and then spot Beaver Island in Washington Harbor. This is a beautiful stretch of the trail as it continues

A hiker enjoys Grace Creek Overlook from Feldtmann Lake Trail.

to hug the harbor shoreline to provide constant views of the water and Beaver Island for almost a mile.

At 1.1 miles or almost directly across from the Beaver Island boat dock, the trail swings sharply inland and begins climbs. Quickly the trail swings west again and in a half mile steeply climbs almost 100 feet of what remains of the actual Greenstone Ridge. At 1.7 miles of the trailhead you break out on a rocky crest with views of Lake Superior and the mouth of Grace Creek to the west. You quickly pass an unmarked spur that leads 30 yards south to a rocky knob known as Grace Creek Overlook. Here you have an even better view of the Island's interior including Grace Creek and Feldtmann Ridge. On a clear day sharp eyes will spot the fire tower on Feldtmann Ridge.

You follow the open ridge for another quarter mile, enjoying good views most of the time, and then make a sharp descent off the ridge. Eventually the trail bottoms out and swings south and 3.2 miles from the trailhead comes to a footbridge across Grace Creek.

Beyond Grace Creek Feldtmann Lake Trail becomes a level walk in the woods for easy hiking. You descend only briefly at 3.7 miles to cross a small stream that can easily be dry in late summer. The trail resumes as a level walk with little to look at beyond the trees around you. But there are often signs of moose, from prints and droppings to nibbled aspen saplings and trees where bulls have rubbed the bark off in the fall. The fact you have a chance of seeing the animals themselves brings a heightened awareness to this trail and makes up for the lack of scenery.

At 4.6 miles you skirt a low bluff that was once the ancient shoreline of Lake Superior. On a windy day it's possible to hear the surf of the Great Lake here but you never see water. Within a half mile, or 5 miles from the trailhead, you break out in a large grassy clearing, the largest since descending the ridge before quickly returning to the woods.

A little more than 2 miles from the Feldtmann Lake Campground, the trail swings to a more easterly direction, and the slices of sky seen through the trees tells you Rainbow Cove is not that far away to the west. During much of this stretch, you hike below ancient shorelines formed when glaciers kept Lake Superior at a higher level. The old beaches are an interesting formation as they create the impression you are hiking below Feldtmann Lake.

Within 0.5 mile of the campground, the trail finally breaks out at a view of Feldtmann Lake, a beautiful body of water crowned in the southeast corner by Feldtmann Ridge and Sugar Mountain off in the distance. The campground is on the west end of the lake and has individual and group campsites, pit toilets, and a red sandy beach, where you can often find moose or even wolf tracks. It's a pleasant place to set up camp, and its popularity limits backpackers to two consecutive nights here through most of the summer. The posted trailhead to Rainbow Cove, a 0.8-mile walk, is nearby (page 176).

Feldtmann Lake to Siskiwit Bay
Distance: 10.3 miles

This is a long but scenic hike, one that backpackers should begin early in the day and not try to rush through. You begin by skirting the south side of Feldtmann Lake for 1.5 miles from the campground to the base of the Feldtmann Ridge. For the first half of this stretch, the trail swings close enough to the lake for eager anglers to bushwhack to the shoreline. Feldtmann is one of the finest northern pike lakes in the park.

This pleasant stroll ends when the trail reaches the base of the

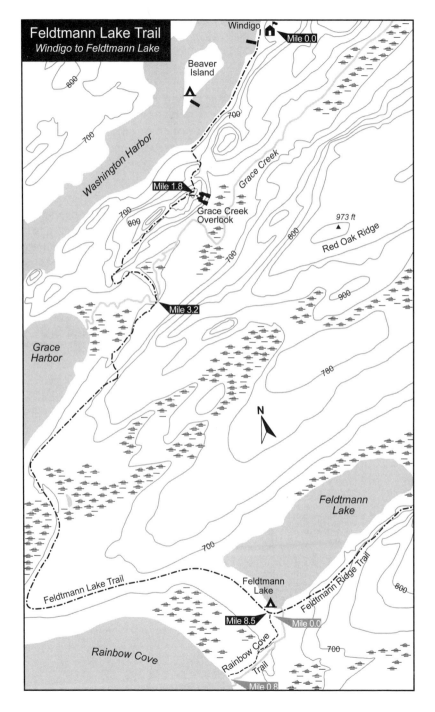

Feldtmann Lake Trail
Windigo to Feldtmann Lake

Windigo
Mile 0.0

Beaver Island

Washington Harbor

Grace Creek

Mile 1.8
Grace Creek Overlook

973 ft
Red Oak Ridge

Mile 3.2

Grace Harbor

N

Feldtmann Lake

Feldtmann Lake Trail

Feldtmann Lake

Feldtmann Ridge Trail

Mile 8.5

Mile 0.0

Rainbow Cove

Rainbow Cove Trail

Mile 0.8

A backpacker picks raspberries near the Feldtmann Tower.

ridge and begins to climb sharply. When seen from a distance, the high bluffs have a reddish color in places, caused by the conglomerate rock they are composed of, and are topped by what often appears to be a single line of white pines. You climb 240 feet in elevation but it's worth it. You top off on a knoll with an incredible view and shaded by three pine trees. Below is Feldtmann Lake, including any moose feeding at its east end, while to the west is Grace Harbor and Rock of Ages Lighthouse. To the east you can see Siskiwit Bay and the Greenstone Ridge. Be careful not to venture too close to the edge of the ridge: Much of the rock is undercut at the drop-off.

More views to the north are enjoyed as the trail continues along the ridge, dipping and climbing on a gradual ascent to the Feldtmann Tower. The trail winds through stands of birch and mountain ash and openings caused by the forest fire of 1936, and at one point you emerge at a swamp with signs of beaver activity around it. You skirt a small pond and then dip into a shaded cut where a stream flows out of a scenic red rock bowl as a small waterfall.

Once across the stream, the trail begins its ascent to the tower, a climb that is not nearly as hard as the first one up the ridge. The tower is reached 4.8 miles from Feldtmann Lake Campground or 5.5 miles from Siskiwit Bay Campground, and the halfway point is the perfect place for an extended break or lunch. The elevation is 1173 feet, and the structure puts you above the surrounding trees for one of the best views on Isle Royale. You can gaze for miles in every direction and see almost the entire western half of the Island, including Big Siskiwit Swamp, Sugar Mountain, and the Greenstone Ridge; to the northeast, Siskiwit Bay, Lake Halloran, and even Malone Bay are visible.

After departing from Feldtmann Tower, the trail descends into the trees but quickly resumes climbing again, and in 0.5 mile you break out on an open ridge. The stone foundation and collapsed logs are remains of the original fire tower.

The trail departs the ruins and begins the mile-long but rarely steep descent off the ridge. You bottom out at a remarkably level and straight path that passes through patches of thimbleberry, almost shoulder high at times. Much of the remaining trail was originally part of a network of logging roads that extended into the swamps of Big Siskiwit River. The logging activity took place from 1935 until the fire of 1936. During that time, lumbermen cut a number of roads toward the swamp, and from the top of Feldtmann Ridge some are still visible as changes in vegetation.

This road stands out, however, because loggers built it on a terrace that was an old Lake Superior beachline. At one time in the formation of Isle Royale, Big Siskiwit River Valley was under water as a part of Lake Superior. Feldtmann Ridge and much of the land to the south was an island.

Within 2 miles of the descent, the trail begins to parallel Lake Halloran. The lake is located only 0.5 mile to the south but is never seen from the trail.

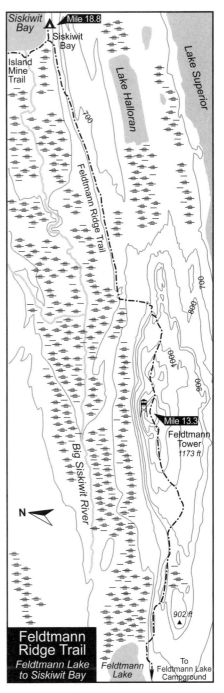

A backpacker follows Siskiwit Bay beach on the way to Island Mine.

The last leg of the trail leaves the patches of thimbleberries and ferns and enters a forest for a refreshing change and finally crosses a large grassy clearing just before reaching Siskiwit Bay. The large clearing was the site of the logging camp responsible for all the swamp roads and then a Civilian Conservation Corps (CCC) camp after the fire of 1936. A little farther on, just before entering the campground, you arrive at the junction with the Island Mine Trail.

The Siskiwit Bay Campground is a pleasant spot to spend a night or even an extra day. Some have dubbed the spot "Riviera of Isle Royale" as it features warmer air and water temperatures than much of the park and has long stretches of red sandstone beach. The campground has two shelters, group and individual campsites, tables, and pit toilets, and a large dock. The only drawback is the campground's popularity with sport fishermen, who troll the nearby reefs for lake trout, and it can become crowded during the summer.

Siskiwit Bay to Greenstone Ridge
Distance: 4.8 miles

The 4.8-mile Island Mine Trail is an historical walk through much of the park's past. You could probably hike from Siskiwit Bay to the Greenstone Ridge in 3 hours or spend an entire day exploring artifacts in brush alongside the trail.

From the junction with the path to Feldtmann Ridge, the trail departs north toward the Greenstone Ridge. At this point, the Greenstone Ridge Trail lies 4.7 miles north and Feldtmann Lake Campground is 10.2 miles west via the Feldtmann Ridge Trail.

The first 1.5 miles of the Island Mine Trail are a beautiful walk circling the west end of Siskiwit Bay. Most of the time the trail is just inside the brush off the beach. If hiking in the early morning, you might want to walk along the beach to check the sand for fresh tracks and avoid getting soaked by wet underbrush.

The trail crosses bridges over two forks of the Big Siskiwit River and then arrives at Senter Point. The trail crosses the neck of the point, which was used by the Island Mine Company in the 1870s to store their explosives. Just before reaching the beach on the north side of the point, you can hike a short way toward the end of the point and see the remains of the stone powder house.

North of Senter Point, the trail follows the beach to its northern end, where it swings northwest and moves inland. At this spot the mining company built a town that housed the workers and serviced the mines 2 miles north. The company constructed a wagon road from the camp to the shafts where 213,245 pounds of refined copper were mined from 1873 to 1875.

The trail follows the bed of the wagon road for the next 2 miles – and this makes for easy hiking. The first mile inland is a level walk through wet lowlands, mostly of spruce and fir. After a stepping-stone crossing over a small creek, the trail begins to climb.

Those interested in the trees and forests of the Island will marvel at this spot, because the creek marks a transition in the makeup

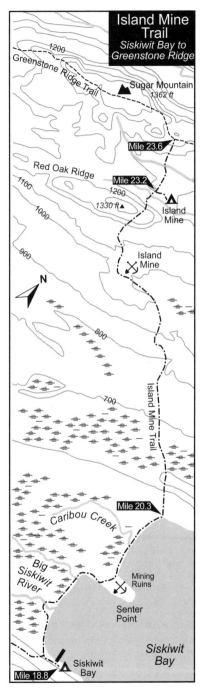

of the woods. The trail leaves the cool, moist valley of spruce, fir, and paper birch and climbs a south-facing slope exposed to long hours of sunlight. In this dry, warm terrain sugar maples and northern red oaks take over as the predominant trees.

The trail climbs for 0.75 mile where it passes an old well, climbs for another 0.75 mile, and arrives at the Island Mine. What remains are large piles of rock tailings, evidence that this was the second largest mining operation on the Island. If you poke around the area, be careful of the old shafts and pits.

The wagon road ends here, and the trail departs from the mining site as a much narrower and more rugged path. It makes its steepest ascent of the day before reaching the crest of Red Oak Ridge at an elevation of 1280 feet. The ridge is appropriately named and from mid- to late September will be ablaze in fall colors. If enough leaves have fallen, you might also get a glimpse of Siskiwit Bay to the southeast.

The trail descends the ridge through a series of switchbacks and quickly bottoms out at a stream. Island Mine Campground is just on the other side.

Some backpackers spend the evening at Island Mine Campground (see chapter 6); others prefer to hike the Greenstone Ridge to Windigo, mostly a downhill trek. To reach the Greenstone, hike through the campground and follow the trail as it ascends to the crest of the ridge. At the junction with the Greenstone Ridge Trail, 0.4 mile from the campground, the Windigo Ranger Station is 6.5 miles to the west and South Lake Desor Campground is 5.1 miles to the east on the Greenstone Ridge Trail.

❖   ❖   ❖   ❖

ROCK HARBOR AND LAKE RICHIE TRAILS

Distance: 13.2 miles
Hiking time: 2-3 days
High point: 726 feet
Rating: easy to moderate

The Rock Harbor Trail is probably the busiest trail in the park. In midsummer, when the Ranger III pulls in, a stampede often results as hikers scurry down the trail to secure a shelter or campsite at Three Mile or Daisy Farm Campground. If just stepping off one of the ferries, you can hike to Three Mile Campground in 1.5-2 hours while Daisy Farm Campground is another 2.5-3 hours away.

A camp fox at Daisy Farm Campground.

The first half of the Rock Harbor Trail is an incredibly scenic walk along the bluffs of the shoreline, with constant views of the water. The second half to Moskey Basin swings inland and is more difficult but not nearly as laborious as it used to be. This section has been rerouted in recent years to make it an easier walk over the rocky terrain.

Rock Harbor Lodge to Three Mile
Distance: 2.8 miles

At Rock Harbor, follow the path through the campground to the beginning of the trail. It is a well-worn footpath that departs from the campground and winds through spruce forest for 0.5 mile before breaking out on a bluff above the water. From this point to Three Mile Campground, the Rock Harbor Trail is one of the most scenic hikes on the Island. It stays within view of the water and islands most of the time but is constantly crossing flat rock outcroppings. If the sun is out and the bugs are not too bad you can take a nap on any one of them, falling asleep to blue sky, even bluer Lake Superior and green islands.

You do need to watch for cairns on the open ridges, and be careful when it is raining as the rock surfaces can get extremely slippery. At one point the trail dips to waterline and passes an islet just offshore, then climbs back into the woods and arrives at a sign for Suzy's Cave 1.8 miles from Rock Harbor Lodge.

The cave is actually an inland sea arch carved by waves when the shoreline of Lake Superior was higher. Named for Suzy Tooker, a fisherman's daughter who often played here, the cave is 80 yards to the north and provides an excellent viewing point of the Rock Harbor waterway. Beyond it the trail remains in the forest briefly and returns to the edge of the shoreline for the remaining mile to Three Mile Campground.

The campground is pleasant, situated right off the shoreline, and a much quieter alternative to the one at Rock Harbor. But being so close to where the *Ranger III* unloads its passengers, it can fill up fast during the summer, the reason for its 1-night limit. Three Mile has eight shelters, group and individual campsites, pit toilets, and, most unusual, two docks. From either you can listen to the water lap onshore in the evening or watch the waves rush through the gaps between Inner Hill Island and Mott Island across Rock Harbor.

Three Mile to Daisy Farm
Distance: 4.4 miles

At 0.2 mile west of Three Mile Campground, the trail arrives at the junction of the side trail to Mount Franklin. The scenic mountain peak lies 2.3 miles to the north on the side trail, Daisy Farm Campground is 4.2 miles west along Rock Harbor Trail.

The trail departs from the junction and continues its course along the side of Rock Harbor. At one point it reaches a rock bluff, and across the channel you can see the cove on Mott Island where the NPS barges are docked. After another mile or so, you stand opposite the NPS headquarters on Mott Island.

Shortly after that, the trail passes the remains of the Siskowit Mine, 1.9 miles from the Mount Franklin junction. One of the first mines on Rock Harbor, Siskowit Mine operated from 1847 to 1855 and during that time produced almost 200,000 tons of copper. Several fenced-off shafts and the stone foundations of former buildings the miners built are in the area. Caution should be used when investigating the shafts.

The rest of the walk to Daisy Farm Campground is a very pleasant and level 2.3 miles. At times the trail crosses clearings where you should be able to see Caribou Island Campground and then Rock Harbor Lighthouse and Edisen Fishery. Roughly a half mile from

Daisy Farm, you will spot the long dock jutting out in the channel.

Daisy Farm was originally a company village known as Ransom that was built in the late 1840s by the Ohio & Isle Royale Mining Company to service its nearby copper mines. In 1903, the area was still an open field when the operators of Rock Harbor Lodge purchased it to grow vegetables for their guests and locals. The area became known as Daisy Farm when the operation grew more daisies than tomatoes or cucumbers.

From 1935 to 1941, the CCC also had a camp here with up to 156 men who worked on docks, fire fighting and the construction of the park headquarters on Mott Island. When not working the men could entertain themselves at two horseshoe pits, a badminton court and a boxing ring. At one point they even had a piano and a three-piece orchestra and Isle Royale's only billiards table. Even as late as the early 1960s Daisy Farm was still more of an open field.

Today Daisy Farm is a shoreline campground that falls in the same category as those at Rock Harbor and Windigo. It's a very popular spot to spend a night or even a couple of days and, consequently, has a lot of traffic. Only a small portion of the field can be detected as a forest of saplings

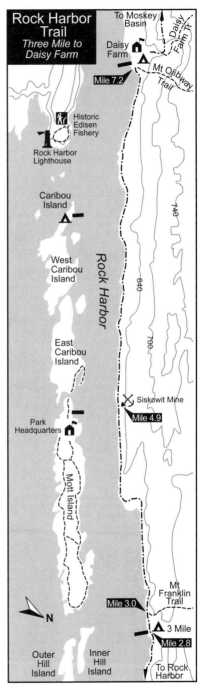

Backpackers leave Suzy's Cave, a popular stop along the Rock Harbor Trail.

and trees has returned the site to a more natural appearance.

The campground has 16 shelters (often taken by early afternoon) and group and individual campsites. Backpackers will also find pit toilets, tables, and even a covered picnic area. A ranger stationed here gives evening talks during the summer. There is also a large dock, from the end of which you can see Moskey Basin to the west, Mott Island to the east, and the restored Edisen Fishery straight across.

Daisy Farm to Moskey Basin
Distance: 3.9 miles

The Rock Harbor Trail follows the Daisy Farm Trail as it departs from the campground and heads northwest for the Greenstone Ridge. After 0.2 mile, you arrive at the junction where the two trails split. Daisy Farm Trail heads northwest, reaching the Greenstone Ridge Trail in 1.7 miles.

The Rock Harbor Trail heads west and a quarter mile from the junction passes an unmarked path that wanders a few yards up a rock outcrop. You should take a moment to walk to the edge. It 's the only glimpse of Moskey Basin you'll have on the entire trek.

For the next 2 miles the trail begins its up-and-down course over one rocky crest after another. A few times it dips down into wooded terrain, only to break out and ascend

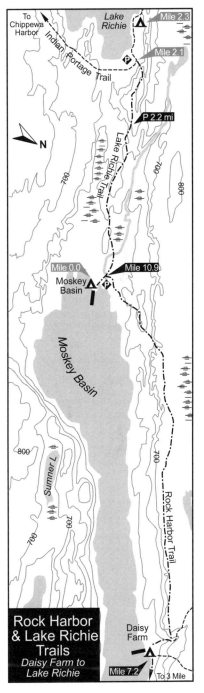

another bare, rocky crest. Keep sharp eyes out for rock cairns because the trail is easy to lose. There are a few steep climbs and descents but none of them are long.

Within 2.5 miles from the junction with Daisy Farm Trail, you finally leave the open ridge and descend into the trees. In another 0.2 mile you cross the only creek in this stretch. The trail ascends from the creek and in the final 0.7 mile climbs over a low, forested ridge before descending gently to the junction with the Lake Richie Trail.

At this junction, Lake Richie lies 2 miles to the west, Daisy Farm is 3.7 miles to the east, and Moskey Basin is 0.2 mile across an unnamed stream to the south. Moskey Basin is a beautiful campground situated right off the well-protected waters at the end of Rock Harbor. It offers six shelters, group and individual campsites, pit toilets, a large dock, and some spectacular sunrises that are well worth leaving a warm sleeping bag in the morning. Climb the rocky bluffs above the dock for an incredible view down the length of Rock Harbor.

From Moskey Basin you can hike the Lake Richie Trail to the Indian Portage Trail, which takes you to the Greenstone Ridge. Once on the Greenstone you can head east to return to Rock Harbor in 1-2 days or continue west and reach Windigo in 2-3 days.

Lake Richie Trail
Distance: 2.1 miles (Moskey Basin to Indian Portage Trail)

From the junction with the Rock Harbor Trail north of the unnamed stream, the Lake Richie Trail departs west and runs parallel to the stream for a short distance. It passes a bog, crosses another stream and then winds through a spruce-fir forest for almost a mile. At this point it emerges at its first rock outcropping.

Here the path along the bare rock is almost as distinguishable as if trail signs were posted; it's smooth and pale pink from thousands of boots trudging across it. The trail follows the contour of the ridge for a spell, descends, and then climbs a second ridge. It stays on the crest of this outcropping even longer, reaches a high point of 726 feet, and then descends into the woods. The Lake Richie Trail officially ends at the junction with the Indian Portage Trail, which heads south for 4.1 miles to Chippewa Harbor Campground.

From the junction, you wander west on the Indian Portage Trail for another 0.2 mile to the shoreline of Lake Richie. The Lake Richie Campground is another 0.1 mile farther on.

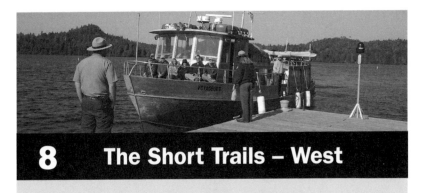

8   The Short Trails – West

❖ *Huginnin Cove Loop*
❖ *Windigo Nature Trail*

Windigo is a nice place if you have a spare day and it doesn't have to be spent hanging around the camp store. The west end of the Island does not feature the number of short trails found in the vicinity of Rock Harbor, but there are still opportunities for overnight excursions and pleasant day trips.

The most popular side trail is Huginnin Cove Loop, a 9.4-mile round trip out of Windigo. The trail loops through the northwest corner of the park and passes through the secluded and scenic Huginnin Cove, a good place to watch a sunset. The other and longer alternative for an overnight trip is a hike out to Feldtmann Lake, known for its heavy concentration of moose. It's a one-way trip of 8.5 miles along Feldtmann Lake Trail (see chapter 7) and, unless you have 3 days, backtracking the route the next day. But many feel seeing Rainbow Cove alone is worth it.

In a rented canoe, a day can be spent exploring Washington Harbor, including the shipwreck *America*, which can be seen from the seat of the boat (see chapter 14). If all you have is a half a day left on the Island, there are the overlooks on Minong Ridge Trail (6 miles round-trip) Feldtmann Lake Trail (3.6 miles round-trip), the Wendigo Mine ruins on East Huginnin Cove Trail (4.2 miles round-trip) or the short Windigo Nature Trail.

❖   ❖   ❖   ❖

HUGINNIN COVE LOOP
Distance: 9.4-mile round trip from Windigo
Hiking time: 4-6 hours
High point: 847 feet
Rating: Moderate

The loop to Huginnin Cove is an excellent overnight trip that requires 2-4 hours of hiking each way. There are a few ridges to climb, mostly along the West Huginnin Cove Trail, but overall this route can be enjoyed by most park visitors - especially those looking for an opportunity to view a moose.

The loop winds past and through a number of swamps, wetlands, and small ponds, all excellent places to encounter the large mammal. The best bet in seeing one is to camp at the cove and that evening return to a high perch overlooking one of the swamps passed through during the day.

From Windigo head east past Washington Creek Campground to the junction with the Greenstone Ridge Trail. You actually begin on the Minong Ridge Trail, but not to worry, it's the easiest portion of this challenging route. The trail winds through the woods and in 0.6 mile from the junction descends to cross Washington Creek. Next to the bridge a small gauging station houses instruments used to measure the flow of the creek.

Just up the trail on the other side of Washington Creek, is a posted junction where West Huginnin Cove Trail heads northwest to reach the campground in 3.1 miles. Although it's probably a much-debated topic, many feel the loop is easier to hike by first following the East Huginnin Cove Trail. The posted trailhead to this path is another 0.6 mile east along the Minong Ridge Trail.

East Huginnin Cove Trail
Distance: 3.3 miles

The trail departs from the Minong Ridge Trail and within 0.3 mile comes to the posted Wendigo Mines, which operated from 1890 to 1892. A short spur leads to what remains today; one wall of an old cabin that's still standing and an assortment of metal work, mostly railroad lines. You depart the ruins, climb steadily along an

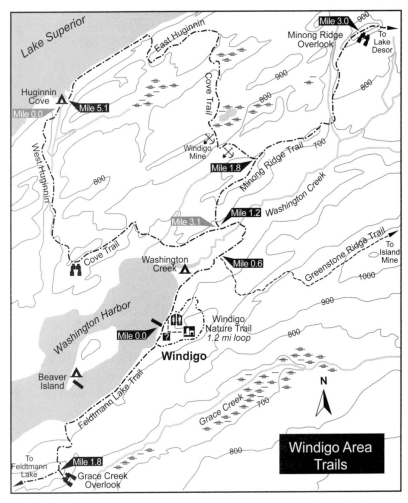

Windigo Area Trails

old railroad bed and a mile from the East Huginnin Cove Trail junction arrive at the log remains of a second mining cabin.

After surveying 8000 acres in Washington Creek basin in 1890, the Wendigo Copper Company set up the Island's most elaborate townsite, Ghyllbank (population 135), at the present site of Windigo. Two miles inland, the company also built the settlement of Wendigo, which consisted of log cabins and two boarding houses for the miners. Neither one lasted very long because the company never found enough copper to support the operation. The failure of the Wendigo mines marked the end of the mining era at Isle Royale.

Within a few hundred yards of the second cabin the trail

An old cabin, part of the mining ruins along the East Huginnin Cove Trail.

descends to a small pond anchoring a vast wetland and uses a board-walk to skirt its north side before climbing away. Needless to say, this is an excellent spot to look for wildlife. You swing to the west and follow a rocky bluff for a spell, where you sense you're getting close to Lake Superior from the gentle breezes blowing through the trees, cooling you off and keeping the bugs at bay.

At 1.5 miles from the East Huginnin Cove Trail junction you begin a steady descent and arrive at your first view of Lake Superior within a 0.3 mile. Here the trail swings sharply west and follows the rugged bluff above the lake, providing many fine views of the water. At times you can look down the steep cliff at the shoreline of jumbled boulders and understand why this is the start of a treacher-ous segment for kayakers circumnavigating the Island. Even landing at Huginnin Cove can be tricky.

For almost a mile, you tread along a shoreline bluff with the Great Lake on one side and the rocky bluff and outcroppings tower-ing above you on the other. The trail, meanwhile, threads its way between huge boulders that came tumbling down so long ago that they now have trees growing on top of them, Eventually you dip away from Lake Superior and come to the junction with West Hugin-nin Cove Trail reached 3.3 miles after departing the Minong Ridge Trail or 5.1 miles from Windigo.

Huginnin Cove Campground is just beyond. The dock is no longer standing, having caved in to the pounding waves of Lake

Superior, but the spot is as secluded and beautiful as any along the Island's north shore. The campground offers a handful of individual sites, a pit toilet and a small beach loaded with so much washed-up debrie that several sites feature comfortable driftwood benches. It is

The Steamship *America*

Isle Royale's most popular shipwreck is the *America*, a steamship that carried passengers and freight to the Island for 26 seasons from 1902 to 1928. Built in 1898, the *America* was originally a day-excursion vessel that cruised between various Michigan ports and Chicago. But in 1910-1911 she was extended by 18 feet to 182.6 feet and equipped with 12 staterooms forward of the engine room.

Her final voyage began on June 6, 1928 when she departed Duluth enroute to Thunder Bay. That night she sailed from Grand Marias to Isle Royale to drop off a number of passengers and then in the pre-dawn darkness of June 7 departed from Washington Harbor.

At this point the captain turned command of the vessel to his first mate and returned to his stateroom. Within minutes the *America* hit a reef in the North Gap, ripping open a small hole in her bottom and quickly sinking. There were 31 crew and 16 passengers onboard but the only casualty was a dog that was tied up near the stern.

One reason for the shipwreck's popularity is because its bow is only 4 feet below the surface. This makes it not only popular among scuba divers but also paddlers who can view it in the crystal clear waters of Lake Superior from the seat of their canoe or kayak. In Rock Harbor Lodge there is the America Dock at Snug Harbor. The ship frequently docked here and today one of its lifeboats is on display.

The America Dock at Snug Harbor in Rock Harbor.

also possible to scramble over the rocks and climb to the cove west of Huginnin, where large flat rocks make ideal sites for sunbathing.

West Huginnin Cove Trail
Distance: 3.1 miles

Near the campground, next to Huginnin Creek, is the junction of the two trails to the cove. From here Minong Ridge Trail is 3.1 miles away, while the Windigo Ranger Station is 4.3 miles.

The West Huginnin Cove Trail begins with an immediate ascent. You climb for almost a half mile until you top off at 813 feet, where it's possible to see the other side of a large ravine that Huginnin Creek flows through. From this lofty perch, the trail descends until it reaches the stream at the bottom and crosses over to the east side of the ravine.

You skirt the wet area and along the way pass a small pond. Anywhere along here a moose could pop out, and for those camping at the cove, this is a good area to stake out at dawn or dusk in hopes of spotting one. At 1.5 miles from the campground, the trail swings away from the low-lying swamp and steeply climbs out of the ravine.

This is the first of three ridges that must be climbed on the way back to Washington Creek. The third is also a good ascent but along the way you're rewarded with some nice views of Washington Harbor. The trail skirts the lightly forested side of the last ridge and then merges into the Minong Ridge Trail, just up from Washington Creek. It's a 1.2-mile walk west to reach the Windigo Ranger Station.

❖   ❖   ❖   ❖

WINDIGO NATURE TRAIL
Distance: 1.2 miles
Hiking time: 30 minutes
Rating: Easy

This trail is an easy walk near Windigo and good for loosening up your legs before the boat ride home. The self-guiding trail features 11 interpretive posts that cover everything from lichens and moose droppings to island geology and succession. Pick up the accompanying brochure at the ranger station and head to the store for the start of the loop. Post 11 is a junction where you can either return to the store, passing a moose enclosure along the way, or drop down to where the Feldtmann Lake Trail runs along Washington Harbor.

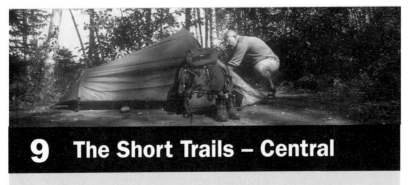

9　The Short Trails – Central

❖ *Indian Portage and Lake Mason Trails*
❖ *Ishpeming Trail*
❖ *East Chickenbone Trail*
❖ *Hatchet Lake Trail*

These trails are in the central portion of the park and are usually combined with portions of the Greenstone and Minong Ridge routes for a variety of week-long tramps. Because they all basically run north to south, they involve hiking over several ridges. The trails can be tiring at times, but none of them is near the difficulty of the Minong Ridge Trail.

The Indian Portage Trail, from Chippewa Harbor to McCargoe Cove, is the only path on the Island that comes close to going from shore to shore. It is a scenic trail and a fisherman's delight as it winds through the northern inland lakes, touching the waters of Richie, LeSage, Livermore, and Chickenbone. Paddlers portaging their boats across the park use the 10.8-mile route extensively.

The Ishpeming Trail winds 7 miles from Malone Bay Campground around the west end of Siskiwit Lake to Ishpeming Point on the Greenstone Ridge. The trail allows hikers to reach Malone Bay, one of the park's most pleasant campgrounds. To avoid backtracking, some backpackers use intra-island transportation to start out at Malone Bay and then plan on 4-5 days to return to Rock Harbor.

The East Chickenbone Trail is a 1.6-mile route along the back (east) side of the lake, from the Greenstone Ridge Trail to the Indian

Portage Trail just outside McCargoe Cove. The Hatchet Lake Trail is a 2.6-mile path that connects the Greenstone Ridge to the Minong Ridge.

❖   ❖   ❖   ❖

INDIAN PORTAGE AND LAKE MASON TRAILS

Distance: 11.1 miles
Hiking time: 7-10 hours
High point: 800 feet
Rating: Moderate

Originally Native Americans used this route to portage their birchbark canoes across the Island, from Chippewa Harbor to McCargoe Cove. The Civilian Conservation Corps built this trail in the 1930s, and today the northern portion from Lake Richie to McCargoe Cove is frequently used by anglers, hikers, and canoeists. Not as many hikers travel along the southern portion, because it dead-ends at Chippewa Harbor.

The path traverses just about every type of terrain found in the park. Along the way you will pass lakes, swamps, and beaver ponds. You will climb ridges and pass through dense forest and sections still scarred by the 1936 fire. Most hikers arrive on either the Greenstone Ridge or the Rock Harbor Trail and head north or south on Indian Portage at this point. To accommodate all hikers, the trail will be described from Lake Richie north to McCargoe Cove and Lake Richie south to Chippewa Harbor.

Lake Richie to McCargoe Cove

Distance: 6.7 miles

The Lake Richie Trail runs from Moskey Basin Campground to a junction with the Indian Portage Trail, 0.2 mile from the east shore of Lake Richie. At this point the Greenstone Ridge Trail lies 3.6 miles to the north, and Chippewa Harbor Campground is 4.1 miles to the south.

From this junction, the Indian Portage Trail heads west to the shoreline of the lake and follows it closely for a short way. It then arrives at the Lake Richie Campground, situated up in the woods off the lake.

The campground has individual and group campsites and pit toilets. The campsites are up on a bluff tucked away in the woods

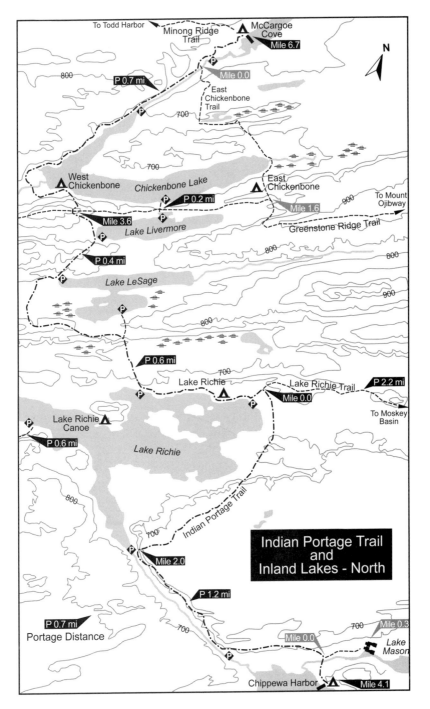

Indian Portage Trail
and
Inland Lakes - North

The campground in Chippewa Harbor features views of Lake Superior.

with no view of the lake below. This isolates campers from the traffic on the trail but also from any wind off the lake. At times bugs can be a problem. The campground is a favorite among visitors because it offers excellent shore fishing nearby and a good chance to spot moose in the early morning or at dusk.

From the campground, the trail winds for almost a mile on a bluff that forms the north shore of the lake. This is an easy walk and a very pleasant section with excellent views of Lake Richie and the small islands that dot it.

Eventually, the trail swings north, climbs and levels out on a ridge, and then drops down to the swamps bordering Lake LeSage. At this point, You arrive at a junction with a side trail that wanders over a small hump to the shore of Lake LeSage. Canoeists and kayakers take the side trail and put-in to paddle straight across the lake.

Hikers follow Indian Portage Trail as it swings to the west where it crosses a ridge, drops to a swamp, and then crosses another low ridge. You eventually descend to another low-lying wet area that is crossed by planking and swing toward the second arm of Lake LeSage. Follow the short portage that departs to the south here for a scenic view of the lake's other half or do a little shore fishing for northern pike.

The trail departs from Lake LeSage and gently climbs a ridge. From the ridge you drop sharply to the portage marker for Lake Livermore and then use planking to skirt the marshy west end of the lake. The trail swings away from the lake and ascends the Greenstone Ridge. The climb is a gentle one considering this, after all, is the backbone of the Island.

At the top of the Greenstone, a major junction offers many choices. The Hatchet Lake Campground is 7.7 miles to the west, and Daisy Farm Campground is 7.7 to the east on the Greenstone Ridge Trail. North at the end of the Indian Portage Trail is McCargoe Cove, 3.1 miles away.

After departing from the ridge, the trail drops rapidly for 0.2 mile to West Chickenbone Campground on the shores of the lake (see chapter 6). It winds through the campground along the shoreline and heads into a swamp at the west end of the lake. The trail crosses the marsh and stream along a planked walk and then returns to the lakeshore.

You then follow the northern arm of Chickenbone for a beautiful hike. On a clear day the lake is a canvas of blue, highlighted by loons and beavers swimming by and painted turtles sunning themselves along the shore. The trail always keeps the lake in sight as it follows the arm to the portage sign at the end.

You depart from the lake and follow Chickenbone Creek to McCargoe Cove, passing a handful of old beaver dams along the way. The arm, creek, and cove are in a depression that was part of an ancient geologic fault cutting diagonally across the Island. For the most part, the trail stays up on the ridge of the fault but comes near the stream twice for a little up-and-down hiking in the final mile.

The trail passes two junctions 0.7 mile from McCargoe Cove. The first is with the East Chickenbone Trail, which leads back 1.6 miles to East Chickenbone Campground. The second immediately follows and is the put-in spot for paddlers portaging a boat.

Just before arriving at the cove, you'll pass a flat sandy area to the right. This was caused by the stamp mill the miners built 40 yards up the ridge. The mill crushed ore that was brought from the mines 0.8 mile away on a narrow-gauge railroad and disposed of the stamp sand by allowing it to wash down the hill The open area was later used by the miners as a stable for their horses. Little remains today that shows the intense activity that characterized the area a century ago.

Lake Richie to Chippewa Harbor
Distance: 4.1 miles

The other half of Indian Portage Trail departs south from the junction with the Lake Richie Trail and immediately swings away from the lake. Here it remains for about 2.0 miles, climbing over the old burned slopes of the 1936 forest fire. The trail eventually shifts toward the southwest and descends to a junction with a short spur to the portage marker on the southern arm of Lake Richie.

From the lake's arm, the trail follows the drainage creek along the ridge to the beginning of Chippewa Harbor. Twice along this mile-long stretch the trail makes two substantial climbs, topping out the second time at a rock outcropping. From this high perch, you can view the stream below or even catch a glimpse of Lake Superior to the south.

From the outcropping, it's 0.3 mile to the portage marker, with most of it a steady descent off the ridge. After passing the portage, the trail climbs another ridge, reaches the top, and levels out. Here, the trees are still scrubby from the 1936 forest fire. On your left (or to the northeast), a pond is surrounded by a large marsh, a good place to look for moose feeding. From the ridge, the trail swings due south and begins its descent to Chippewa Harbor.

Right before reaching the campground, the trail passes the side trail to Lake Mason. The side trail takes about 10 minutes one way and is an easy 0.3-mile walk to the rock bluff that overlooks the west end of the lake.

Chippewa Harbor Campground is another favorite for hikers because its four shelters are situated high above the water, with a good view of the harbor. The narrow entrance from Lake Superior, surrounded by rugged bluffs and small islands, is especially beautiful. The campground also has individual and group campsites, pit toilets, tables, and a dock.

❖   ❖   ❖   ❖

ISHPEMING TRAIL
Distance: 7 miles
Hiking time: 4-6 hours
High point: 1377 feet
Rating: Moderate to difficult

The trail winds from Malone Bay Campground to Ishpeming Point on the Greenstone Ridge, ascending three major ridges along the way. The steady climb makes this hike more difficult than most trails on the Island.

Ishpeming Point, which to the Ojibway Indians meant "heaven," is the second highest point on the Island (1377 feet). The views

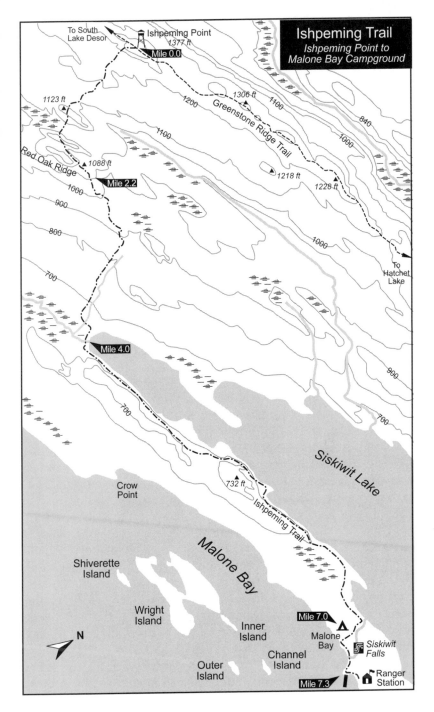

To South
Lake Desor
Ishpeming Point
1377 ft
Mile 0.0

Ishpeming Trail
*Ishpeming Point to
Malone Bay Campground*

1123 ft

1306 ft

840

1200

Greenstone Ridge Trail

1100

1100

Red Oak Ridge

1088 ft

Mile 2.2

1218 ft

1228 ft

1000

900

800

1000

700

To
Hatchet
Lake

Mile 4.0

900

700

700

Siskiwit Lake

732 ft

Ishpeming Trail

Crow
Point

Malone Bay

Shiverette
Island

N

Wright
Island

Inner
Island

Mile 7.0

Malone
Bay

Siskiwit
Falls

Channel
Island

Outer
Island

Mile 7.3

Ranger
Station

A backpacker patiently waits for dinner time in a backcountry campsite.

are uninspiring, however, because only the west end of Siskiwit Bay is visible through the trees. From this point, South Lake Desor and Hatchet Lake campgrounds, both approximately 4.0 miles away, lie to the west and east, respectively.

The Ishpeming Trail departs from the lookout tower and immediately begins its long descent from the Greenstone Ridge. At times the trail is steep and wanders over bare rock surfaces, where the path is easy to lose. After 0.75 mile, the trail finally bottoms out, crosses a planked swamp and small stream and begins a steep ascent.

This time the trail peaks at 1123 feet before descending off the ridge into a marsh still scarred by the 1936 forest fire. After passing through the wet area, the trail begins to climb again and reaches 1088 feet on Red Oak Ridge. From the top, there are views of Siskiwit Bay while the forest changes from yellow birch to large stands of sugar maple, northern red oak, and white pine.

The trail gradually descends from the ridge by heading east before turning south for the western end of Siskiwit Lake. It continues to drop for more than a mile from Red Oak Ridge before leveling out in birch-aspen forest. After another 0.75 mile, the trail crosses a boardwalk through a swamp and over a small stream and then quickly arrives at a second stream.

This one connects Mud Lake with Siskiwit Lake and is crossed on a wooden bridge. From the middle of the bridge, you can view the western end of Isle Royale's largest lake. The trail departs from the bridge and immediately swings to the east. It follows the lakeshore for another 3 miles through a paper-birch forest.

There is an occasional view of the lake through the trees, and halfway along the shore you climb over a small knoll. The trail passes a marsh right before arriving at the Malone Bay boat landing on Siskiwit Lake. Near the landing, a stream forms Siskiwit Falls, a rather uninspiring cascade, before emptying into Malone Bay.

On this narrow bridge of land between the lake and the bay is Malone Bay Campground, one of the most beautiful in the park. On the bayside there are smooth pebble beaches to comb and views of the long reefs that separate the bay from Lake Superior as well as Isle Royale Lighthouse (1875) on Menagerie Island. The campground features five shelters, group and individual campsites, pit toilets, tables, and a dock. A ranger is stationed there for the summer, and the latest weather report is posted on his cabin. Siskiwit Lake is known for its wide variety of sport fish, including brook and lake trout.

❖   ❖   ❖   ❖

EAST CHICKENBONE TRAIL
Distance: 1.6 miles
Hiking time: 1-2 hours
High point: 720 feet
Rating: Easy to moderate

The East Chickenbone Trail begins 0.7 mile from McCargoe Cove Campground and swings around the east end of Chickenbone Lake to the Greenstone Ridge Trail. It is often combined with part of the Greenstone and Indian Portage trails for a pleasant 7-mile day hike around Chickenbone Lake from McCargoe Cove.

From the junction with Indian Portage Trail, this trail dips to cross Chickenbone Creek on a wooden bridge, and then makes a steep climb out of the geologic fault trench. It follows the ridge top for a 0.5 mile, dipping and climbing, before descending to a beaver pond.

The trail skirts the west end of the small pond along a boardwalk that puts you only an arm's length away from the beaver dam and then swings sharply to the east and follows the other side. You leave the pond and swing south, where the trail descends to another marshy area with planking before breaking out at the eastern edge of Chickenbone Lake. Again the trail uses planking to skirt the marshy end of the lake and then climbs a ridge to East Chickenbone Campground, passing a spur along the way that campers use to obtain water from Chickenbone Lake.

East Chickenbone is located in the trees west of the trail. It has three individual sites and a group site but none have a view of the lake below. Gathering water at camp is a steady descent to the lake below. From the junction to the campground, East Chickenbone Trail ascends briefly before arriving at the junction with the Greenstone Ridge Trail (see chapter 6).

❖   ❖   ❖   ❖

HATCHET LAKE TRAIL
Distance: 2.6 miles
Hiking time: 2-3 hours
High point: 1057 feet
Rating: Moderate
Map: Page 76

This trail connects the Greenstone Ridge with the Minong Ridge and is used by many hikers out of Windigo who want to walk only a portion of the rugged Minong Ridge Trail. It is also the side trail to Hatchet Lake Campground for backpackers hiking along the Greenstone Ridge.

From the ridge, the trail descends sharply from its high point of 1057 feet until it arrives at a junction near the shore of Hatchet Lake in 0.3 mile. A spur heads 0.2 mile west to the Hatchet Lake Campground (see chapter 6) while Hatchet Lake Trail departs in the other direction to wind its way past the eastern end of the lake.

At first the trail remains close to the southern shoreline but then climbs the hillsides above the lake. Within 0.5 mile the trail swings north and crosses a stream that empties into the east end of Hatchet Lake. From here you climb a forested ridge and follow it for 0.2 mile before descending to a second stream in an open marshy area. This stream is often dry by late summer.

The trail returns to a forested setting and in 0.5 mile or 2.3 miles from the junction to the campground makes its final ascent to the junction with the Minong Ridge Trail. From here you can hike to either Todd Harbor (1.4 miles) or Little Todd Harbor (5.3 miles) for the night (see page 78). Before embarking for Little Todd Harbor, keep in mind that the Minong Ridge is a rugged trail where there is little water available.

10   The Short Trails – East

❖ *Tobin Harbor Trail* ❖ *Mount Franklin Trail*
❖ *Daisy Farm and Mount Ojibway Trails*
❖ *Lane Cove Trail* ❖ *Lookout Louise Trail*
❖ *Stoll Trail* ❖ *Mott Island Circuit Trail*
❖ *Raspberry Island/Lighthouse Loop Trails*

Some backpackers never leave the Rock Harbor area. They make their way down the waterway, stopping for a couple of days at every campground. They explore only a limited section of the Island but rarely run out of places to hike or things to see.

The trails in and around Rock Harbor and the eastern end of the park offer the most variety of any on Isle Royale. Not only do they vary in difficulty, but also their views and scenery vary from the bare crest of the Greenstone Ridge to the panorama from Lookout Louise to the half-hidden beaches and coves on Mott Island.

Two scenic loops from the Rock Harbor Lodge can be turned into leisurely day hikes. For an afternoon of craggy coastline and pounding Lake Superior surf, the Albert Stoll Memorial Trail travels east of the lodge to the end of Scoville Point. To the west of the lodge, you can combine the Tobin Harbor Trail with a portion of Mount Franklin and Rock Harbor trails for a 6.5-mile trek that rarely leaves the shoreline.

Much more rugged is the 5.1-mile loop along Daisy Farm, Mount Ojibway, and a portion of the Greenstone Ridge Trail. The

Day hikers chat with a pair of backpackers on the Mount Franklin Trail.

walk involves climbing several ridges, including the Greenstone, but the views from Mount Ojibway Lookout Tower are excellent. So are those from Mount Franklin, which can be seen on an overnight trek to Lane Cove Campground. This trip involves a one-way hike of 6.9 miles from Rock Harbor along the Mount Franklin and Lane Cove trails to the secluded Lane Cove Campground.

One other option for those staying at Rock Harbor Lodge is to rent a canoe at the camp store or join a day cruise to combine hiking with a trip on the lake. With either water transportation, several days can be spent hiking Lookout Louise, Mott Island, Raspberry Island, or the Edisen Fishery/Lighthouse Loop. More experienced hikers can even arranged to be dropped off at Hidden Lake for an 11-mile trek back to Rock Harbor Lodge or McCargoe Cove a 15.4-mile trek back (see chapter 5).

❖   ❖   ❖   ❖

TOBIN HARBOR TRAIL

Distance: 3 miles
Hiking time: 1-2 hours
High point: 640 feet
Rating: Easy
Map: Page 72

Although the trail rises and dips a little, it is a wide, dry, and easy path to hike. Many hikers view the Tobin Harbor Trail as a more scenic alternative to the stretch from Rock Harbor Lodge to Three Mile Campground. It can be combined with the Rock Harbor Trail for a 6.5-mile day hike or can be shortened to 3.8 miles by cutting over at Suzy's Cave.

You pick up the trail from the paved path that leads to the housekeeping units and immediately pass a spur to the seaplane dock on

Tobin Harbor. From here, Tobin Harbor Trail gently rises west and passes a side trail that leads back to group campsites in the Rock Harbor Campground. You continue to climb and dip gently along the shoreline of the harbor in a most pleasant stretch. The ground is soft and well shaded by a thick canopy of birch, and fir, while views of the waterway and the small islands that dot it never go away.

The junction to Suzy's Cave is 1.8 miles from the seaplane dock junction. The cave, an inland sea arch created when Lake Superior was at a higher level, is a short climb away on the ridge. From the junction to the cave, the trail levels out somewhat and follows the shoreline until it comes almost to the end of the harbor. You finally leave the water here, wander less than a quarter mile through the forest, and arrive at the junction with the Mount Franklin Trail.

At this point you can head north on the Mount Franklin Trail and reach the Greenstone Ridge Trail (1.5 miles) or hike south 0.5 mile and reach Rock Harbor Trail near Three Mile Campground.

❖   ❖   ❖   ❖

MOUNT FRANKLIN TRAIL
Distance: 2 miles
Hiking time: 60-90 minutes
High point: 1074 feet
Rating: Moderate

This trail is often the entry ramp for hikers tackling the Greenstone Ridge Trail. From a junction with the Rock Harbor Trail, it runs 2 miles to the ridge, passing the Tobin Harbor Trail along the way. Mount Franklin, with its incredible views, is actually 0.3 mile west on the Greenstone Ridge Trail.

The Mount Franklin Trail begins 0.2 mile west of Three Mile Campground at a well marked junction along the Rock Harbor Trail. The trail begins by immediately climbing a ridge and then descends to a boardwalk through a wetland. On the other side you pop out at the junction with the Tobin Harbor Trail, 0.5 mile from Three Mile Campground. To the east on the Tobin Harbor Trail lies the spur to Suzy's Cave (1.2 miles) and Rock Harbor seaplane dock (3 miles).

You continue north, following considerable planking and using a bridge to cross Tobin Creek and the wetland it flows through. The trail then swings east to climb a low grassy ridge, followed by a descent to skirt a pond and the north side of a marsh. Beyond the pond the trail suddenly curves north and begins its steep climb of the

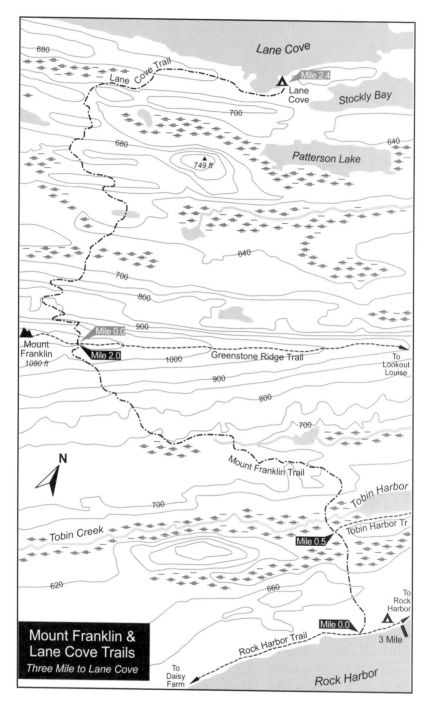

Lane Cove

Lane Cove Trail

Mile 2.4

Lane Cove

Stockly Bay

700

680

749 ft

Patterson Lake

640

680

640

700

800

900

Mile 0.0

Mount Franklin
1080 ft

Mile 2.0

1000

Greenstone Ridge Trail

To Lookout Louise

900

800

700

N

Mount Franklin Trail

Tobin Harbor

700

Tobin Harbor Tr

Tobin Creek

Mile 0.5

620

660

To Rock Harbor

Mile 0.0

3 Mile

**Mount Franklin &
Lane Cove Trails**

Three Mile to Lane Cove

Rock Harbor Trail

To Daisy Farm

Rock Harbor

Greenstone Ridge. The hike to the junction of the Greenstone Trail is a knee-bender that lasts for half mile and ascends more than 300 feet. Watch for an occasional cairn where the trail crosses bare rock bluff as it is easy to lose it in such spots.

If you are heading for Lane Cove, stash your pack after reaching the junction and scramble 0.3 mile west to the top of Mount Franklin. The high point is not really a mountain but, rather, a rock bluff along the Greenstone Ridge, but at 1080 feet, it's high enough to provide a superb view of Canada and the north side of the Island. Officially, Mount Franklin Trail ends here and becomes the Lane Cove Trail, which winds 2.4 miles to the secluded Lane Cove Campground. West on the Greenstone is Mount Ojibway (2.8 miles); the junction of the trail to Lookout Louise is 4.8 miles east.

❖   ❖   ❖   ❖

LANE COVE TRAIL

Distance: 2.4 miles
Hiking time: 2-3 hours
High point: 1074 feet
Rating: Moderate to difficult

Lane Cove Trail and the campground at its north end are the only avenue hikers have to the Five Fingers of Isle Royale, that special area of long, narrow bays and fiordlike coves. This is an excellent first-night destination out of Rock Harbor for any backpacker hiking the Greenstone and anxious to escape the bustle of campgrounds like Daisy Farm. The trek from Rock Harbor to Lane Cove is 5.9 miles, via the Tobin Harbor Trail.

At the junction near Mount Franklin, Lane Cove Trail begins with an immediate and steep descent of the Greenstone Ridge, using a series of switchbacks to climb down off the Island's backbone. Early in the descent you're rewarded with views of the Island's north shore. You bottom out in a half mile where at the base of the ridge, the trail uses boardwalks to cross wetlands and a stream before climbing over a low wooded ridge

Several more low ridges follow in the next mile. At 1.8 miles from the Greenstone Ridge junction, you skirt an old marsh, cross it at one end, and climb what appears to be just another ridge. Actually what you're traversing is a 3000-year-old beachline of Lake Superior. From the ancient shoreline, the trail descends to the current one and emerges at Lane Cove and winds around it to the campground.

The shoreline campground is one of the few along Lake Superior without shelters and offers only individual campsites and pit toilets. But the area is beautiful as you view the entire cove or gaze beyond its narrow mouth to the tree-studded islets north of Belie Harbor. On a clear day, this is also one of the few campgrounds where you can view Canada from your tent site.

❖ ❖ ❖ ❖

DAISY FARM AND MOUNT OJIBWAY TRAILS
Distance: 5.1 miles
Hiking time: 3-5 hours
High point: 1136 feet
Rating: Moderate

For those hiking the loop from Daisy Farm Campground, it is easier to hike clockwise by first walking the Daisy Farm Trail, which reaches the Greenstone Ridge at one of the ridge's lowest points. Most hikers, eager to see the views from the lookout tower, immediately tackle the steeper Mount Ojibway Trail.

From Daisy Farm, the 1.7-mile Mount Ojibway Trail gently climbs to the top of Ransom Hill. It moves through spruce-fir forest, passes an open meadow thick with thimbleberry bushes and finally peaks at the top of the hill. The 880-foot hill provides many hikers with their first view of the Greenstone Ridge to the north, and even the lookout tower for those with sharp eyes.

You descend the north slope through a paper-birch forest before leveling out and crossing a swamp created by Tobin Creek via a bridge 0.9 mile north of Daisy Farm. The trail climbs a second ridge, levels out, and then makes its final ascent up the Greenstone Ridge. Portions of the climb can be steep. But halfway up, the trees thin out and you are rewarded with views of the south shore.

The trail ends at the lookout tower. Built in 1962-1963 as a fire lookout, the tower's role has since changed from smoke detection to sampling air for pollutants. Because of the Island's remote location, the air here should be clean to offer a prime sampling site to scientists. That's the theory anyhow, but on days when the wind is blowing from the north that distinct odor you often smell is from the pulp mills in Canada. The tower is no longer manned, but a display explains its use and the solar panels on the side that power the air-quality instruments. The best part of the structure is climbing its steps for one of the best views on the Greenstone Ridge. You can see

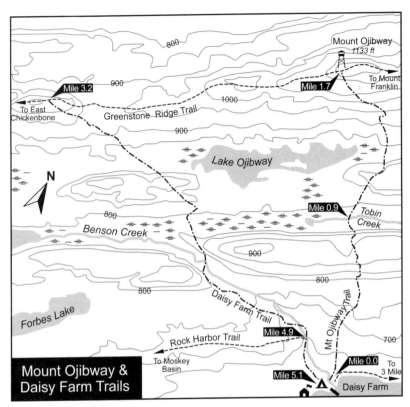

Mount Ojibway &
Daisy Farm Trails

a good portion of the Island's eastern half, including both shorelines and Angleworm Lake and Lake Benson to the southwest.

Next to the tower is the junction with the Greenstone Ridge Trail (see chapter 6). From this point, the junction of the Mount Franklin Trail lies 2.8 miles to the east; West Chickenbone is 7.5 miles to the west.

Greenstone Ridge to Daisy Farm

Distance: 1.9 miles

The Daisy Farm Trail arrives at the Greenstone Ridge at a relatively low point, making it one of the easiest routes to the ridge. The path begins from the junction with the Greenstone Ridge Trail 1.5 miles west of the Mount Ojibway Lookout Tower.

From here it gently descends off the ridge for 0.5 mile where at first you hike over rock outcroppings while enjoying a glimpse or two of the south shore. You quickly reenter the forest and eventually bottom out at an interesting marsh surrounding a large rock out-cropping. The dead trees in the middle of the pond are a clear indication of beavers. A boardwalk crosses a small stream here that flows to Angleworm Lake. The trail departs from the pond and climbs over a low ridge to a second swamp, where marsh vegetation such as bog laurel, Labrador tea, black spruce, and tamarack can be spotted.

The trail leaves the swamp, climbs over the western tip of Ransom Hill, and crosses a bridge over Benson Creek about a mile from Daisy Farm Campground. The trail skirts a ravine along the western side of the creek. You can't actually see the creek below in the steep and wooded ravine but you sense it's down there. Soon you're crossing and re-crossing Benson Creek on two bridges to arrive at the junction with the Rock Harbor Trail to Moskey Basin (3.7 miles).

From the junction, the trail winds into Daisy Farm Campground, one of the largest on the Island (see chapter 7).

❖   ❖   ❖   ❖

STOLL TRAIL
Distance: 4.2 miles round trip
Hiking time: 1.5-2.5 hours
High point: 639 feet
Rating: Easy

This easy loop trail begins at Rock Harbor Lodge and travels 2.0 miles east to rugged Scoville Point. The trail winds back and forth between the forest and the shoreline, where craggy bluffs and sharp cliffs are testimony to Lake Superior's power and persistent erosion.

You pick up the Stoll Trail near the dining room where its trailhead is located just beyond the last set of lodge rooms. The trail begins in the woods but quickly breaks out to views of Rock Harbor, where a few benches have thoughtfully been placed. In a quarter mile you arrive at a high bluff overlooking the last few islands that form the harbor. An exhibit describing the ancient copper pit is nearby, 0.7 mile from the start, with several pits visible.

Just past the exhibit, a junction of a side trail intersects the return loop on the Tobin Harbor Trail. Stoll Trail continues east, stays near the shoreline for another 0.7 mile, passes scenic views of the rugged bluffs and cliffs on the Lake Superior shoreline, and finally reaches the rocky end of Scoville Point. At the tip of the point is a memorial to Albert Stoll, Jr., The Detroit News reporter who campaigned to turn Isle Royale into a national park.

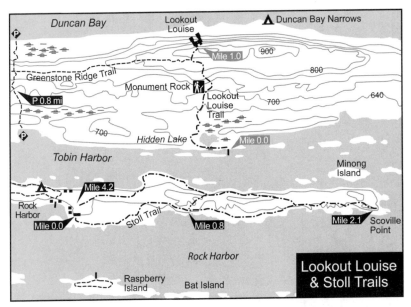

Duncan Bay
Lookout Louise
▲ Duncan Bay Narrows
P
Mile 1.0
900
Greenstone Ridge Trail
800
Monument Rock
640
P 0.8 mi
Lookout
Louise
Trail
700
700
Hidden Lake
Mile 0.0
Tobin Harbor
Minong
Island
▲ Mile 4.2
Rock
Harbor
Mile 0.0
Stoll Trail
Mile 0.8
Mile 2.1 Scoville
Point
Rock Harbor
Lookout Louise & Stoll Trails
Raspberry
Island
Bat Island

The point is named after an 1840's copper prospector and is a mix of craggy rock shoreline, juniper brushes and a few scraggily pines. It's a beautiful spot where you can sit on the rock bluffs, soak in the sun and watch the boaters on their way to Rock Harbor.

From Scoville Point, you backtrack 0.6 mile to where the return loop trail divides. The return is, for the most part, a soft path through the woods with the best views and even a bench occurring after the cutoff spur. Although the scenery is not nearly as dramatic as Scoville Point, the final mile along Tobin Harbor is still an enjoyable walk. At one point you can look down Tobin Harbor and see the seaplane dock and, if you're timing is good, possibly witness the float plane taking off. The remains of Smithwick Mine can also be seen, right before the trail reaches the lodge.

❖ ❖ ❖ ❖

LOOKOUT LOUISE TRAIL
Distance: 1.0 mile
Hiking time: 45--60 minutes
High point: 880 feet
Rating: Difficult

By renting a canoe or joining the *MV Sandy* at Rock Harbor Lodge, you can combine a water cruise with hiking and visit some

A backpacker takes in the sweeping view from Lookout Louise.

of the most interesting spots on the Island. One of them is Lookout Louise, a favorite among visitors. The lookout spot provides the most spectacular view in the park, but most of the 1-mile trail is a straight, uphill climb.

If you rent a canoe, launch it from the seaplane dock. You can then paddle across Tobin Harbor and follow the shoreline east for a mile to the Hidden Lake dock, located just past a group of three islets. The trail departs from the dock, hugs the shoreline, and then swings inland to wind around Hidden Lake. Keep your eyes open around this small lake because moose often visit its mineral licks.

From the swamp around the lake, you begin a steady climb up, moving into forest and soon passing huge boulders along the side of the trail. A few are more than 6 feet tall and many have trees or a carpeting of moss growing on top. But it's hard to miss the largest boulder on this trek. Within a half mile from the trailhead you reach

Monument Rock, a high, stone pinnacle carved by Lake Superior waves when that body of water was at a higher elevation. The landmark is actually a pair of stone towers that rise dramatically above the surrounding pines.

The trail skirts the monument, breaks out at an open hillside with views of Tobin Harbor to the south, and then arrives at the junction with the start of the Greenstone Ridge Trail. From here it is a 0.1-mile climb to Lookout Louise, while the junction of the Mount Franklin and Lane Cove trails is 4.8 miles to the west.

The final 0.1-mile stretch to Lookout Louise is all climbing before you break out of the trees to the famous viewing point. Succession and young saplings have eroded the panorama over the years but it's still a spectacular sight. Stand on a rock if you have to and look to the east to see the jagged peninsulas at the end of Duncan Bay. To the northwest is the rest of the bay along with Five Finger Bay, Belle Harbor, and even Amygdaloid Island. Due west you can see the Greenstone Ridge extend along a good portion of the Island, and then look down: You will nervously realize that Lookout Louise is the crest of an incredibly steep bluff.

❖   ❖   ❖   ❖

MOTT ISLAND CIRCUIT TRAIL

Distance: 2.6 miles
Hiking time: 1-2 hours
High point: 640 feet
Rating: Easy
Map: Page 109

A full day can be spent paddling from Rock Harbor Lodge to Mott Island and hiking the beautiful and little-used Mott Island Circuit Trail (see map on page 109). The paddle is about 4 miles from Rock Harbor, and in good weather conditions you can plan on 2-3 hours each way.

Mott Island, the site of park headquarters, is a bustling place during the summer, as rangers, maintenance people, and trail crews pass through. Don't land your canoe at the main dock. Paddle to the beach on the east side of the harbor and secure your boat there.

The circular trail begins and ends near the seaplane dock. By staying to the left, the trail follows the protected shore of Rock Harbor, rising and dipping gently.

It stays in the forest for the first mile, with only quick views of the water through the trees before passing the cove where the NPS docks its supply barges.

From here the trail hugs the coast and winds through a handful of small coves with views of the harbor and nearby islands. At one point, it dips down to a pebbled cove at the northeast tip of Mott Island, where you can see Lorelei Lane - the narrow channel that divides the outer islands to the east.

At this point, the trail swings east and follows the Lake Superior shoreline, passing more coves. If the afternoon is sunny, you can sunbathe on the smooth, bare rocks along the shore. Eventually, the trail swings back to its beginning near the seaplane dock.

❖   ❖   ❖   ❖

RASPBERRY ISLAND/LIGHTHOUSE LOOP TRAILS

Distance: 0.8 mile
Hiking time: 30 minutes
High point: 646 feet
Rating: Easy
Map: Page 137

Distance: 0.4 mile
Hiking time: 15 minutes
High point: 640 feet
Rating: Easy
Map: Page 109

These two spots are not really hiking trails but are interesting places to visit. Raspberry Island is directly across Rock Harbor Lodge and is an easy paddle on a calm day. The self-guiding trail has interpretive markers that point out the unusual plants and other features of this excellent little bog.

Across from Daisy Farm Campground are the Edisen Fishery and the 0.5-mile loop to the old Rock Harbor Lighthouse (see map on page 109). Pete Edisen operated this well-preserved fishery for more than 50 years. From the fishery, the short trail that winds to the lighthouse begins. Enroute it passes the burial site of an Island miner.

The lighthouse was built in 1855 to guide boats into the harbor during the mining era. It was abandoned after 1879 but later occupied as a summer home around 1900 and then by the families of fishermen working the Island. The NPS stabilized the structure and turn it into a maritime exhibit. The return loop departs from the lighthouse, follows the cliffs overlooking Middle Islands Passage, and returns to the fishery.

For those who don't want to paddle to Raspberry Island or the Rock Harbor Lighthouse, the park concessionaire offers guided day trips to both spots aboard the *MV Sandy*.

Isle Royale

By Paddle

Kayakers and canoers arriving at Rock Harbor after their paddle through the Isle Royale backcountry.

11   The Inland Lakes – North

❖ *Rock Harbor* ❖ *Lake Richie*
❖ *Lake Lesage* ❖ *Lake Livermore*
❖ *Chickenbone Lake* ❖ *McCargoe Cove*

Distance: 20 miles (Rock Harbor to McCargoe Cove)
Paddling time: 2-3 days
Portages: 5
Longest portage: 2.2 miles

There may be 165 miles of footpaths, but for many visitors each summer Isle Royale is a paddler's park. Paddling allows you to cover more area and carry more gear and, from the seat of a canoe in the middle of a lake, gives you a clear and different view of the Island. Plus many believe it's an easier method of travel in the wilderness – even with the portages.

The disadvantages of choosing the boat over the boot is that you must have a canoe or kayak and pay an additional charge for ferrying it to the park and back. And it's possible you may be holed up somewhere because of foul weather and rough water. No matter how hard it rains, on foot you can always pack up and hike out – not true when paddling.

But the key difference for many is that more often than not paddling is the only way to seek out the park's isolated corners. And that type of experience is priceless in today's crowded world.

The water routes of Isle Royale are not difficult. Most are well protected and are strung together by short, though not-always-level, portages. Backpackers interested in paddling must have previous canoeing or kayaking experience. This is no place to learn how to handle a boat, but with the right preparation, equipment, and route, the Island can be your first extended wilderness trip via the paddle.

Almost all paddlers arrive at Rock Harbor because Windigo offers limited travel. The most common trip is to paddle Rock Harbor and then cut across the park through the northern inland lakes of Richie, LeSage, Livermore, and Chickenbone to McCargoe Cove. Once in McCargoe, you can weave your way through the bay and coves of the Five Fingers to circle back to Rock Harbor. The trip takes 6-7 days at a comfortable pace.

Always keep an eye out for the water markers placed in the park to assist paddlers. There are two kinds: *portage markers* are long rectangular signs pointed at the top, are stained dark redwood around the outside, and have a large "P" in the middle; *canoe campground markers* are similar, except they display a tent instead of a "P."

❖   ❖   ❖   ❖

ROCK HARBOR
Maps: Pages 109 and 111

The busiest avenue in this roadless park is not the Greenstone, nor even the trail leading west out of Rock Harbor Campground, but Rock Harbor itself – the waterway. The long, narrow harbor, which stretches 13 miles from the North Government Island to Moskey Basin, is a bustling sea-lane during the summer. Everything from *Ranger III* to sailboats and ranger patrol boats can be seen zipping up and down the channel.

It is also the first stretch for most paddlers and a good place to start. The outer islands that form the barrier in front of Lake Superior break up the lake's large, slow-rolling swells and make the harbor calm most of the time. Even if the weather is stormy and Rock Harbor becomes choppy, there are five campgrounds along its shoreline and almost an endless number of coves and inlets to wait out the rough water.

It is a 9.5-mile paddle from Rock Harbor Lodge west to Mokey Basin. Directly across from Rock Harbor Lodge is Raspberry Island (page 140) with its short nature walk (see chapter 10); Tookers Island Campground is 1.5 miles west. This boaters' campground has two shelters, pit toilets, a dock, and a scenic cove nearby. But being close to Rock Harbor Lodge, it is often filled with powerboaters.

A paddler sorts through her gear at a portage to Lake Richie.

If conditions are calm, kayakers can weave their way along the outer islands, passing through narrow gaps and channels. Park rangers strongly recommend that canoeists stay near the main shoreline and away from the open water of Lake Superior as much as possible.

Mott Island is 4 miles from Rock Harbor and is the site of the NPS park headquarters, a scenic 2.6-mile circular trail (see chapter 10), but no campground. Another 1.5 miles west of Mott Island is Caribou Island Campground, on the very western tip of West Caribou Island. This camping spot is a pleasant area with two shelters, a dock, and pit toilets.

On days of southerly winds and rough conditions on Lake Superior, paddlers will know when they are passing Middle Island Passage, the gap between Caribou Island and Rock Harbor Lighthouse: Large swells or even cresting waves funneling into Rock Harbor make the last half mile to Daisy Farm challenging for canoeists. Daisy Farm (see page 109) is 6.5 miles from Rock Harbor Lodge and directly across the harbor from the historic Edisen Fishery (see page 140).

Moskey Basin to Lake Richie Portage
Distance: 2.2 miles
Rating: Difficult
Map: Page 111

Just beyond the popular campground, the harbor narrows and then opens up into beautiful Moskey Basin. Three miles west of Daisy Farm, an easy 1.5-hour paddle away, you come to the end of Rock Harbor and the dock to Moskey Basin Campground. Moskey Basin is the point where many canoeists and some kayakers make their first portage, carrying their boats inland to Lake Richie. Although the Lake Richie Trail is often referred to as a 2-mile portage, by the time you pick your boat out of the water at Moskey Basin and drop it in at Lake Richie, it's closer to 2.2 miles. Either way, it's a loooong portage and, unfortunately, often the first one, when the food bags are the heaviest. The route is not difficult but does wind over two small ridges before reaching the water (for a trail description, see page 112).

❖   ❖   ❖   ❖

LAKE RICHIE
Map: Page 121

Lake Richie is a favorite among paddlers and is an ideal place to spend an extra day. The main body of the lake is broken up by four islands, the largest being Hastings Island, and two arms extend along the western shoreline. The lower arm extends 0.75 mile and is the beginning of the portage trail to Chippewa Harbor.

The upper arm extends northwest almost a mile, and the marker for the Intermediate Lake portage is along the southern side. Near the tip of the peninsula that forms the mouth of the arm is Lake Richie Canoe Campground. The campground was moved here in the late 1980s and features three wooded sites, a pit toilet, and a rocky shoreline from which the northern half of the lake can be viewed. The Lake Richie Campground is on the eastern side, 0.2 mile from the junction of the Lake Richie and Indian Portage trails (see page 120).

The lake is known for pike fishing. All along the shore and between the islands are marshes and weed beds where a northern might be found. Paddlers, of course, have the advantage of fishing in areas away from the trails and untapped by shore fishermen, including the entire western side of the lake. If you are heading toward Chippewa Harbor after mid-summer you can also work the weed beds along the east shore of the lower arm. Avoid doing so any earlier as loons nest in the area.

Lake Richie to Lake LeSage Portage
Distance: 0.6 mile
Rating: Difficult
Map: Page 121

This portage is marked and located on the north shore, directly across from Hastings Island. The route is short but steep: It begins at the shoreline and climbs 100 feet before leveling off on a ridge. The trail then descends to the junction with the Indian Portage Trail around Lake LeSage. Paddlers continue straight ahead, climb another small ridge, and then drop to the Lake LeSage shoreline.

❖   ❖   ❖   ❖

LAKE LeSAGE
Map: Page 121

Lake LeSage is more like two narrow lakes situated side-by-side and connected by a small channel. They are divided by two long peninsulas that jut out into the middle. The portage from Lake Richie leaves you in the middle of Lake LeSage's southern half. It takes about 15 minutes to cross through the channel to the next portage on the northern half.

Or you could take your time and stop for lunch at the tip of the western peninsula. It's a great picnic area, and you can easily beach your canoe or kayak on the small rocky point of land. The channel between the two halves of the lake often is holding pike or perch. Another fishing spot is the south side of the western peninsula.

Lake LeSage to Lake Livermore Portage
Distance: 0.4 mile
Rating: moderate
Map: Page 121

This portage is at the northwest corner of the upper half of LeSage and might be difficult to see at first among all the deadheads that litter this corner of the lake. The trail is short but, like the portage from Lake Richie, steep in places. It departs from Lake LeSage and climbs 80 feet to a ridge before leveling out on top. From the ridge to Lake Livermore, the trail descends so sharply that you might end up bouncing the back of the boat off the ground. The trail arrives at the southwest corner of Lake Livermore.

❖   ❖   ❖   ❖

LAKE LIVERMORE

This long, narrow lake doesn't have the outstanding fishing as those on either side of it: The weed beds are not as extensive, nor do the northern pike seem as big. There are quite a few beaver lodges around it, and they are interesting to paddle past. The marker for the portage to Chickenbone Lake is in a small cove toward the northeast corner of the lake.

Lake Livermore to Chickenbone Lake Portage
Distance: 0.2 mile
Rating: easy
Map: Page 121

This very short portage climbs a little to a low point on the Greenstone Ridge Trail. At this point, the portage passes a serene little waterfall formed by the creek flowing between the two lakes. The portage then dips down to Chickenbone Lake in the middle of the lower arm.

❖   ❖   ❖   ❖

CHICKENBONE LAKE
Map: Page 121

This V-shaped lake is another delightful place to paddle or spend an extra day resting up. The lower arm is about 1.7 miles in length, with West Chickenbone Campground (see page 76), a favorite among campers, at its western end. The upper arm is about 0.75 mile long and heads northeast toward McCargoe Cove.

Wildlife is plentiful around the lake. You can often spot beavers, loons, and possibly even a moose feeding. The best way to observe the wildlife is to paddle along the shore at dusk.

Chickenbone also has excellent fishing for pike, perch, and, if you are skillful enough, walleye. One of the best places to cast a lure is the eastern end of the lower arm.

Chickenbone Lake to McCargoe Cove Portage
Distance: 0.7 mile
Rating: Moderate to difficult
Map: Page 121

A portage marker is on the very end of the upper arm of Chickenbone Lake. The trail is a hilly climb on the ridge along Chickenbone Creek. You climb twice, more steeply if coming from McCargoe Cove, and then within a half mile from the portage marker on Chickenbone Lake you arrive at the posted junction to East Chickenbone Campground (1.6 miles). Around the next bend, within 100 yards, is the portage marker where paddlers can launch their boat into the creek, now wide and deep enough to paddle.

That's most of the time. Some years, however, beaver dams force you to pull a canoe or kayak across the log structures, a challenge in keeping your socks dry. If you continue portaging the trail, the campground is 0.3 mile away and one more ascent up the ridge.

❖ ❖ ❖ ❖

McCARGOE COVE
Map: Pages 121 and 153

This stunning body of water flows from Chickenbone Creek northeast to Lake Superior. The campground (see page 89) is one of the nicest in the park, and the paddle along this waterway is the high point of many trips.

Bluffs enclose McCargoe, but its shore is broken up by a handful of coves and inlets, tempting fishermen to cast a line or moose to stop and feed. It's 2 miles from the campground to Birch Island, the site of an old fishery near the mouth of the cove. John Linklater, the last Ojibway Indian to live on the Island, moved into the fishery in the 1920s. An environmentalist before his time, Linklater guided tourist parties from Birch Island. These trips included hiking from McCargoe Cove to Sargent Lake, where he had canoes stashed, and ended up hiking to Daisy Farm. Linklater died in 1932, but the birchbark canoe he used to paddle around the Island remains in an NPS warehouse in Houghton.

A small campground on the island includes a shelter, a tent site, and a dock. A popular boater's campground, Birch Island is a very scenic place to spend the night, as you can walk across the island to view the mouth of McCargoe Cove and the condition of Lake Superior.

Birch Island blocks the entrance to Brady Cove, a secluded little body of water east of McCargoe. This cove is known for its large but finicky pike. It is also the traditional spot for paddlers to stay and wait for rough water to subside before venturing into Lake Superior.

From Birch Island and Brady Cove, you can paddle around Indian Point into the open waters of Lake Superior to the Five Fingers area at the park's eastern end. *Extreme caution must be used in this section, because the lake can develop slow rollers that sweep to the north side of the Island.* In storms, the north shore is notorious for being the roughest shoreline in the park.

A kayaker loads her boat to depart from an an old fishing camp on the Lake Superior shoreline.

12   The Five Fingers

❖ *Herring Bay, Pickerel Cove & Robinson Bay*

❖ *Amygdaloid Channel, Crystal Cove & Belle Harbor*

❖ *Stockly Bay, Five Finger Bay & Duncan Bay*

❖ *Merrit Lane and Tobin Harbor*

Distance: 13.5 miles (McCargoe Cove to Rock Harbor)
Paddling time: 2-3 days
Portages: 5
Longest portage: 0.8 mile

At the east end of Isle Royale is a collection of long, narrow channels, fiordlike harbors, and secluded coves and inlets loved by all who pass through. They are known as the Five Fingers. Isle Royale is a beautiful place, but for many the Five Fingers are the diamonds at the end of the pendant.

These long, steep ridges that reach into the lake offer rugged beauty, calm water, and visual links to the Island's past. You could easily spend a week exploring this area that covers the far eastern portion of the park and includes seven campgrounds.

Canoes and kayaks are well suited for the Five Fingers. The Lane Cove Trail is the lone footpath into the heart of the east end. Power boaters can travel through much of the Five Fingers but have only four campgrounds with deep-water docks. Paddlers, on the other hand, find calm water, narrow gaps between islands to squeeze through, and a handful of old cabins and camps to explore.

A 3-day paddle is an ideal amount of time to travel from Mc-Cargoe Cove to Rock Harbor while exploring the many coves and islands in between. Many canoeists and kayakers like to spend the first night at either Pickerel Cove or Belle Isle and the second at one of the two campgrounds in Duncan Bay. You can cover this stretch in less time but be disappointed at the end for not having scheduled additional days.

Also remember that Belle Isle, the two campgrounds in Duncan Bay, and the one in Merritt Lane are popular havens for power boaters. Inevitably, you will hear the roar of their engines in these areas or be crowded out of the shelters.

❖   ❖   ❖   ❖

HERRING BAY, PICKEREL COVE & ROBINSON BAY

The only open water most canoeists ever encounter at Isle Royale is the short stretch from the mouth of McCargoe Cove to Herring Bay. It is a nearly 2-mile paddle in which you round Indian Point and head east for the point marking the south side of Herring Bay. Once in Herring Bay it's a mile paddle to the Pickerel Cove portage. Canoeists should use extreme caution and wait for good weather when entering this stretch of Lake Superior. Even on calm days, slow rollers can develop along the north shore of Isle Royale for an extremely difficult paddle in an open canoe.

When the weather is bad and the surf rough, most paddlers sit out the turbulent conditions at Birch Island or Brady Cove. The only other way around it is to paddle into the unnamed cove on the north side of Indian Point, portage across the narrow neck of land on its north side, and paddle to the east end of the next cove. A small island marks the end, and from the mainland shore you can make a half-mile, cross-country portage due east into Pickerel Cove. Without a trail, this is not an easy task. Most parties will need a half day to carry their boats and gear into the Pickerel.

Kayakers, however, have less to worry about and will thoroughly enjoy this stint with Lake Superior. The stretch from McCargoe Cove to Herring Bay is scenic, with grand views of the west end of Amygdaloid Island, the rugged north shore, and mainland Canada off in the distance. There is also something exciting and awe-inspiring about paddling in Lake Superior: Maybe it's the knowledge that the lake is the largest body of fresh water in the world, or perhaps a fascination with its long history of shipwrecks, of which more than

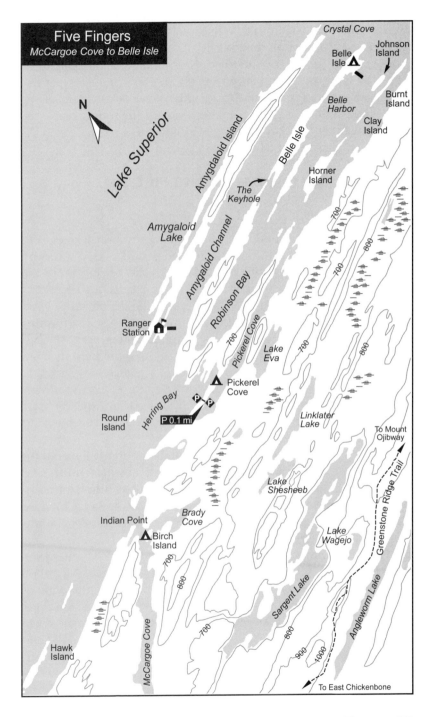

twenty sunk near Isle Royale. Whatever, the short paddle is bound to leave goose bumps on the back of your neck.

By cutting across the mouth of Herring Bay to Amygdaloid Island, you reach the North Shore Ranger Station where park personnel are stationed all summer. Most paddlers choose to enter Herring Bay and make their way to its longest inlet in the southeast corner. Tucked away about halfway along the south shore of the inlet is the portage marker to Pickerel Cove.

Herring Bay to Pickerel Cove Portage
Distance: 0.1 mile
Rating: Easy

The hop, skip, and jump between Herring Bay and Pickerel Cove is the shortest and sweetest portage in the park. The trail is historical: It was originally used to roll barrels of lake herring caught in Pickerel Cove to waiting cargo ships in Herring Bay.

The portage takes you to a spot deep inside the beautiful cove. The long, narrow body of water is stunning and usually bustling with waterfowl. Pickerel Cove Canoe Campground is just to the east of the portage. The little campground, with flat space for only a few tents, is on the ridge overlooking the cove. There are no pit toilets, but the view is great and large, flat rocks are nearby - ideal for lying out in the sun. Although Pickerel Cove is only a short paddle from McCargoe Cove, most canoeists prefer it to Belle Isle because of its isolation.

Once in Pickerel Cove, you could paddle the south shore all the way to Lane Cove or cut through the first gap along the north side. The gap separates the peninsula on the mainland from Horner Island. On the other side of this channel is Robinson Bay, which extends for another 2 miles to the west. To the east is a narrow channel that leads to Belle Harbor.

Or you could paddle straight across Robinson Bay, where you would find a very small opening between two islands. A fiat-bottomed kayak, or possibly a light canoe, might be able to squeeze through, but the water is only inches deep, and overloaded parties will have to get out and carry their boats a few yards across the opening.

On the other side of the opening is a second narrow channel between Robinson Bay and Belle Harbor and still another narrow gap almost straight ahead. This last one is known as the Keyhole and

Kayakers unload their boat at McCargoe Cove.

is wider and deeper because it separates the peninsula on the mainland from Belle Isle. On the other side of the opening is Amygdaloid Channel, a wider and more open waterway than Pickerel Cove or Robinson Bay.

AMYGDALOID CHANNEL, CRYSTAL COVE & BELLE HARBOR

Almost directly across from the Keyhole, midway along Amygdaloid Island's south shore, is a beach where a short trail leads inland. Although unmarked, the trail should not be passed up. It leads through an intriguing sea arch and then to picturesque Amygdaloid Lake. Follow the island's south shore another 1.5 miles west and you'll reach the NPS ranger station, while 2 miles to the east is Crystal Cove and the eastern end of Amygdaloid.

Crystal Cove was once a private residence and then the fishery of Milford and Myrtle Johnson. Milford arrived on the Island in 1906 and until his death spent most of his summers fishing in the park for lake trout, whitefish, and herring.

From Crystal Cove you sprint across Amygdaloid Channel in 15 or 20 minutes to Belle Isle Campground, which features an outdoor grill and covered picnic area. Along with the picnic area, Belle Isle has six shelters, an individual campsite, pit toilets, and tables. The sunrise on a clear morning is especially stunning from this campground. Belle Isle is also an historical spot. The campground was the site of the American Fur Company's first fishing station on Isle Royale in 1837 and fishermen continuously occupied the island until Fred Schofield arrived in 1915. Schofield changed the island's name to Belle Isle and then built a large resort that catered to the grand lake steamers of the time. The shuffleboard courts are still visible as cement slabs, and the pilings of the original dock across from the campground on Belle Harbor are near the present dock. The resort also boasted a golf course and the Island's only swimming pool before closing in 1946.

The islands east of Belle Isle – Captain Kidd, Green, and Dean – can be visited, but use caution when paddling this area. It has little protection from Lake Superior and can turn suddenly rough. Loons also nest in the areas. South of the campground dock is another set of islands that harbor several old fishing camps. Almost straight across are the old fishing camp and boathouses of Johnson Island. The cabin in the camp is still being used and should not be disturbed. There is a lone cabin on Clay Island, and the north shore of Horner Island also once supported a small camp.

Southeast from Belle Isle is Lane Cove, about an hour's paddle away. The stretch between the two is exposed to Lake Superior and can be choppy. After entering the mouth to Lane Cove, the portage marker will be visible to your left, in the southeast corner. The campground in Lane Cove (see pages 133-134) is very scenic and one of the few in this area where you can escape power boaters.

Lane Cove to Stockly Bay Portage
Distance: 0.1 mile
Rating: Easy

This portage comes in a close second with the one at Pickerel Cove as the easiest crossing in the park. Among the trees east of the trail is the site of the old Lane Cove Campground. The portage arrives at the western end of Stockly Bay.

❖   ❖   ❖   ❖

STOCKLY BAY, FIVE FINGER BAY & DUNCAN BAY

Stockly Bay is a long, narrow waterway that extends 1.6 miles northeast into Five Finger Bay. It is well protected, as is much of Five

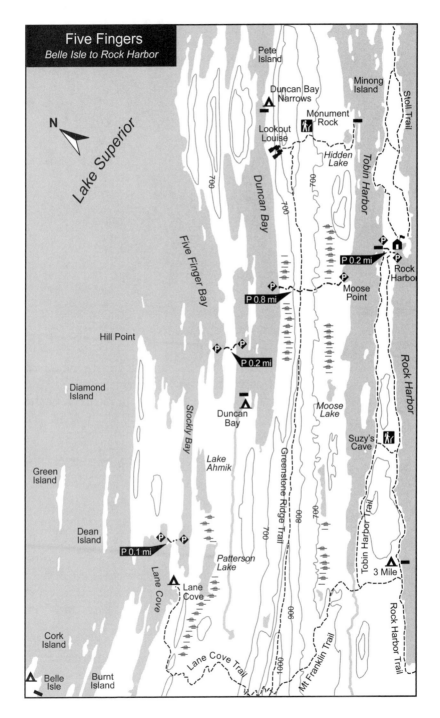

Five Fingers
Belle Isle to Rock Harbor

N

Lake Superior

Pete Island

Duncan Bay Narrows

Minong Island

Monument Rock

Stoll Trail

Lookout Louise

Hidden Lake

Tobin Harbor

Duncan Bay

700

P 0.2 mi

Rock Harbor

P 0.8 mi

Moose Point

Five Finger Bay

Hill Point

P 0.2 mi

Diamond Island

Duncan Bay

Moose Lake

Rock Harbor

Suzy's Cave

Stockly Bay

Green Island

Lake Ahmik

Greenstone Ridge Trail

800

700

Dean Island

P 0.1 mi

Patterson Lake

700

Tobin Harbor Trail

3 Mile

Lane Cove

Lane Cove

900

Cork Island

Burnt Island

Lane Cove Trail

Mt Franklin Trail

1000

Rock Harbor Trail

Belle Isle

A moose pauses from feeding in the Five Fingers region of the park to watch a pair of canoers paddle by.

Finger Bay, but once you venture past the islands in the middle of the bay toward the mouth, the water can be unstable.

By following the south shore of Stockly Bay, you will enter the western edge of Five Finger Bay, round one point, and paddle past an inlet to the west. After you shoot across this inlet and round a second point, you will enter a longer inlet. Head west and look to the south to spot the portage marker to Duncan Bay.

Five Finger Bay to Duncan Bay Portage
Distance: 0.2 mile
Rating: Easy

This portage is twice as long as the last two and involves a little more climbing. Still, it provides paddlers easy passage across land. On the other side, you will come out on Duncan Bay, across from the western end of its largest island. Duncan Bay Campground is a 15- to 20-minute paddle to the southwest.

The campground is at the end of a peninsula that juts out into the middle of the bay. It's a nice place to spend an extra day, especially if you secured one of the two shelters that overlook the water. It also includes an individual campsite, tables, and a dock. Nearby, a small bluff leads to a good view of the western end of the bay.

Duncan Bay, with its many islands and coves, is noted for its fine pike fishing. It takes 1.5-2 hours to paddle east to Duncan Narrows and the campground there. Although not as scenic as the other, Duncan Narrows Campground is still a pleasant spot with two shelters, tables, a grill, and pit toilets. Both campgrounds are popular among power boaters.

From Duncan Bay you can either round Blake Point, a very risky stretch of water, or portage into Tobin Harbor. All canoeists should portage into Tobin Harbor: Blake Point, the eastern tip of the Island, is notorious for being rough, choppy, and unsuitable for small craft. For a 2.5-mile stretch, from the mouth of Duncan Bay until you round the point to Merritt Lane, you will be paddling in open Lake Superior with nothing breaking the surf. The shoreline around Blake Point is composed of steep cliffs with no place to beach and is exposed to wind from all directions. On windy days, the tip of the point can be the scene of wild water with 5- or 6-foot waves sweeping through from several directions.

Duncan Bay to Tobin Harbor Portage
Distance: 0.8 mile
Rating: Extremely difficult

The alternative to paddling Blake Point is considerably safer but no easier on the back. The 0.8-mile portage is by far the most challenging in the park as it climbs 175 feet. In Duncan Bay, the portage is on the south shore almost halfway to Duncan Narrows Campground. The steep climb begins the minute you step out of the canoe, and just pulling the boat out of the water can be a challenge.

The trail begins with a climb, quickly levels, and then makes its steep ascent to the top of the Greenstone Ridge. This is tough hiking along switchbacks, even if you aren't balancing a boat on your shoulders. Within a quarter mile, you top out and pass the junction with the Greenstone Ridge Trail.

On the south side of the ridge, the descent is much milder and eventually you bottom out in a swamp that the trail crosses on a boardwalk. Much to the disbelief of many sore-shoulder portagers, on the other side a small ridge must be climbed before you emerge at the usually quiet waters of Tobin Harbor. The portage ends just northwest of the seaplane dock on the south side of the harbor.

❖   ❖   ❖   ❖

MERRITT LANE AND TOBIN HARBOR

Those who endure the steep portage shouldn't rush across Tobin Harbor just to invade the camp store. Tobin Harbor and Merritt Lane are another scenic part of the Island worth spending the extra time to see.

Within a half mile after rounding Blake Point, Merritt Lane Campground offers a small site with one shelter, one campsite, a dock, a pit toilet, and not much flat land. Don't be disappointed if a fishing party has taken over the place.

From here the paddling becomes interesting due to the islands, coves, and channels you can explore just west of the campground. Eventually, you paddle into an open area where you can view Scoville Point and the mouth of Tobin Harbor.

It is safer to paddle straight into Tobin Harbor to reach Rock Harbor Lodge rather than trying to round Scoville Point. The stretch from the point to Raspberry Island can be considerably rougher than Tobin Harbor.

The mouth of the harbor is partially blocked by several islands, and a dozen cabins are scattered along the shoreline. These are the summer homes of lifetime residents and were built before the Island became a national park.

Paddlers who arrive at Merritt Lane Campground and find it filled need not panic. It is only another 4.0 miles to Rock Harbor Lodge by way of Tobin Harbor.

Tobin Harbor to Rock Harbor Portage
Distance: 0.2 mile
Rating: Easy

As paddlers arrive at the seaplane dock in Tobin Harbor, the last thing on their minds is the portage through Rock Harbor Lodge to the *Ranger III* dock - the final portage before loading the boat on the ferry for the mainland. The walk from Tobin Harbor to Rock Harbor is easy and can be viewed as heroic: Curious lodge visitors, most of whom have rarely ventured beyond Rock Harbor Lodge and the park hotel, are intrigued and quick to inquire about someone carrying a boat on top of his or her head.

It is wise to stake out a shelter or campsite in Rock Harbor Lodge before pirating the camp store.

13   The Inland Lakes – South

❖ *Chippewa Harbor*
❖ *Lake Whittesey* ❖ *Wood Lake*
❖ *Siskiwit Lake* ❖ *Intermediate Lake*

Distance: 18 miles (Lake Richie to Siskiwit Lake and back)
Paddling time: 3-4 days
Portages: 5
Longest portage: 1.2 miles

The southern inland lakes are a breed apart. Most are accessible only to canoeists and kayakers. They require more time and energy to reach than those north of them. They are scenic but do not possess the overwhelming beauty of the Five Fingers.

They do offer one opportunity not found when hiking the Greenstone Ridge Trail or paddling though Rock Harbor: If you have the time and the shoulders willing to carry your boat, you can lose yourself for days at a time in this section of the park. Except for the south shore, nowhere else on the Island is such isolation possible.

Beginning with Lake Whittlesey and continuing with Wood Lake, most of Siskiwit Lake, and Intermediate Lake, this is a paddler's domain. The small number of visitors who bring a canoe or kayak to the park ensure that this section, even during the busiest week of the summer, will always retain a bit of solitude.

The conventional way to reach this area is to paddle Rock Harbor and portage into Lake Richie (see maps on pages 72, 109, and 111). From here you paddle to the lower arm of the lake and endure a second long portage to Chippewa Harbor. After paddling and portaging through Lake Whittlesey, Wood Lake, and Siskiwit Lake, the loop is completed by doubling back through Intermediate Lake, Lake Richie, and Rock Harbor. The trip takes 7-9 days to complete; anything less turns it into a canoe race.

The alternative is to hop on *Voyageur II* and get off at Chippewa Harbor or Malone Bay Campground. This reduces the trip back to Rock Harbor Lodge by 2-4 days. When beginning at Malone Bay, most paddlers choose the more scenic Wood Lake and Lake Whittlesey over the Intermediate Lake route back to Richie.

❖   ❖   ❖   ❖

CHIPPEWA HARBOR

From Lake Richie, paddle south to the end of the lower arm. This part of Lake Richie is an excellent area for pike. At the end of the arm is a portage marker and the mouth of a stream jammed with logs.

For those thinking they might skip the portage and try to paddle down the stream to Chippewa Harbor - don't. Although you could portage your boat around the log jam at the mouth of the stream, the trip would be one frustrating beaver dam after another until you give up and haul your boat up the ridge to the trail.

Lake Richie to Chippewa Harbor Portage
Distance: 1.2 miles
Rating: Difficult

This portage is difficult and long. It follows the ravine the stream cut from Lake Richie to Chippewa Harbor, climbs up and over two high points on the ridge, and ascends 160 feet from its original elevation (for a complete trail description, see page 123). There is little you can do to make it easier except to plan on spending a good part of the day moving camp from Lake Richie to Chippewa Harbor.

The put-in is at the south end of the stream, now a wide and navigable waterway for canoeists and kayakers. A short paddle away you enter Chippewa Harbor, a beautiful sight for anybody who has just struggled over the trail with his or her boat. The water is well protected, and a paddle through the harbor is usually leisurely.

The harbor was the site of one of the Island's largest fishing camps in the early 1900s; several families built cabins and stayed year-round. In the 1930s, there was even a small schoolhouse for the children, which can still be seen by hiking beyond the group camp-

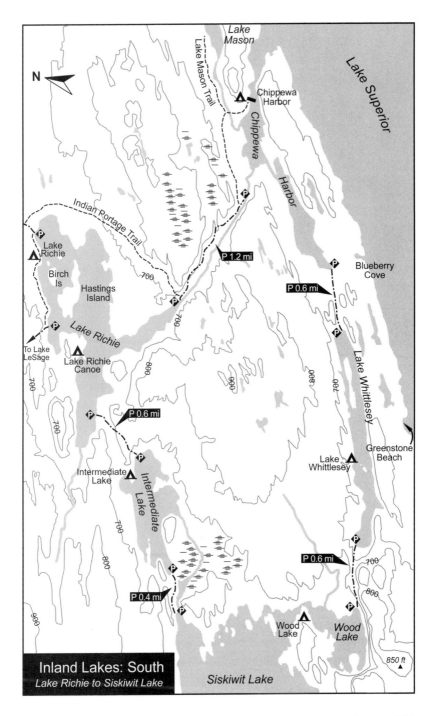

Inland Lakes: South
Lake Richie to Siskiwit Lake

A paddler begins the portage to Chippewa Harbor from Lake Richie.

sites toward the mouth of the harbor. You can also see the remains of the *Ah-Wa-Nesha* as you paddle from the stream south to the Chippewa Harbor Campground. The boat, situated in a small cove of its own along the east shore, was a tourist boat that carried passengers to the Johnson Resort and Trading Post in the mid-1930s, until it was abandoned when the business went bankrupt. Do not paddle near the boat, however, as loons occasionally nest near it.

The campground (see chapter 9), which sits on a bluff overlooking the harbor and its rugged opening to Lake Superior, is an especially enjoyable place for paddlers to spend a spare day. Fishermen can try their luck for pike in any of the many coves and weed beds along the shore. The best spots tend to be deep in the harbor once you pass the narrows heading west.

From the Chippewa Harbor Campground, you paddle back toward the stream to Lake Richie, make a sharp turn west through the narrows, and then emerge into another long body of water. The whole area is scenic, and this paddle is a favorite among canoeists and kayakers. Once in the western half of Chippewa Harbor, look for the portage marker in the southwest corner.

Chippewa Harbor to Lake Whittlesey Portage
Distance: 0.6 mile
Rating: Moderate

The Chippewa Harbor end of the portage looks like it might have been used for hundreds of years by canoeists. Its mouth is carved out of sheer rock and narrows to a sharp V, as if an endless number of birchbark and fiberglass boats have snuggled into it.

The trail is well marked and not difficult but does involve climbing 140 feet with your boat. It leaves Chippewa Harbor and ascends a ridge. After leveling out, the trail descends and climbs a second ridge. From the second ridge, the trail swings more to the west and dips down to the shore of Lake Whittlesey.

LAKE WHITTLESEY

Lake Whittlesey is a narrow body of water that stretches almost 2 miles and is broken up at the east end by a pencil-thin island. Here, more than anywhere else, the isolation of Isle Royale is felt.

Anglers will find the lake a delight - northern pike thrive here. The small coves and weed beds along the shore tend to be the most productive. Whittlesey, however, is known for its walleye population, a fish that challenges the most skillful anglers (see chapter 3). To land a walleye toss jigs and rubber body grubs along shoreline buffs or vertical-jig them over gravel bars or other steep drop-offs.

The Lake Whittlesey Canoe Campground is on the north shore a half mile west of the large island, or almost directly across from a pair of islets. It's a pleasant wooded area with a pit toilet and three individual campsites. From the islets (good spot to jig for walleye), you can spot the canoe campground marker along the shore.

Lake Whittlesey to Wood Lake Portage
Distance: 0.6 mile
Rating: Moderate

From the campground, paddle another 0.75 mile to the end of the lake as it curves slightly to the northwest. Here you will spot the portage marker for the 0.6-mile trail to Wood Lake. Rerouted from its original course, the trail is not as wet as it once was and is easier than the one from Chippewa Harbor: It climbs only 80 feet.

The steepest part of the trail is the beginning as you carry your boat from the waters of Lake Whittlesey to the top of a low shoreline ridge. Before continuing inland, turn around at the top for a final view of Whittlesey. The trail remains level for a while and then begins a gradual descent to the lower level of Wood Lake. Along the way the trail is planked through a cedar swamp.

WOOD LAKE

The portage trail emerges at the southeast corner of Wood Lake,

The shipwreck in Chippewa Harbor, a tourist ship from the 1930s.

a small but delightful place to spend a day. The lake is about a half mile wide along the south shore and tapers off to a narrow gap at the north end which leads into Siskiwit Lake. A handful of small islands combine with many small coves to make the area another excellent place to fish for northern pike.

Paddle north to where the lake narrows and begins to flow into Siskiwit and look to the west for the marker to Wood Lake Canoe Campground. This spot provides ideal conditions for a wilderness camp as it is above the shoreline for a nice view of the lake and the moose that frequently pass through. The campground has three individual sites and a pit toilet. Directly across from the campground is a small cove where more than one pike has been landed.

By scrambling up and over the ridge behind the campsite, you arrive on the other side of the peninsula that separates the two lakes. The views from this spot are among the best in the park because you can survey the eastern half of the Island's largest lake and the Greenstone Ridge off in the distance.

❖   ❖   ❖   ❖

SISKIWIT LAKE

At a length of 7 miles and a depth of 142 feet, this is the longest and deepest lake within the park. It can also be the roughest. Unlike the other well-protected inland lakes, Siskiwit Lake must be entered cautiously. Sudden squalls often blow across the Greenstone Ridge, creating choppy water with 2-foot waves and whitecaps.

It is a 3.5-mile paddle from Wood Lake to the portage to Malone Bay Campground. In ideal weather, it might take you less than 2 hours; if the wind and waves are working against you, twice as long. More than a dozen islands are scattered throughout the lake, most of them located at the east end. Ryan Island has the distinction of being "the largest island in the largest lake on the largest island in the largest freshwater lake in the world."

By staying along the south shore, you paddle through narrow gaps between two islands and the shoreline. The second is Eagle Nest Island, and it is 0.6 mile east of the portage to Malone Bay.

Siskiwit Lake to Malone Bay Portage
Distance: 0.3 mile
Rating: Easy
Map: Page 124

From Siskiwit Lake, it is 0.3 mile to Malone Bay along a level, mostly planked trail that follows the stream between the lake and the bay for much of the way (see map on page 94). The trail splits off at one point, and the left-hand fork leads off to the dock and ranger cabin. The other fork heads straight to the campground shelters.

Some paddlers are dropped off at Malone Bay (see chapter 9), portage their craft over to Siskiwit Lake, and never go any farther the rest of the week. The reason for their contentment is the lake's fishing. The lake contains 17 species of fish but is best known for having the only landlocked population of lake trout in the park.

Power boats are not allowed on Siskiwit, but canoeists and kayakers will find conditions ideal to surface troll for lake trout. Pike and yellow perch can also be landed, especially among the many small islands at the east end.

Many paddlers spend an extra day at Malone Bay Campground before heading back to Rock Harbor Lodge. Interesting day trips in the area include paddling around the islands in Malone Bay. Among them is Wright Island to the west where a fishing camp still stands.

For a combined hiking and boating trip, paddle to the west end of Siskiwit Lake. Here, the stream from Mud Lake empties out and is crossed by the Ishpeming Trail on a wooden bridge. It is only a 4-mile walk from here to Ishpeming Point and the lookout tower on the Greenstone Ridge (see page 124).

Canoeists continuing on to Intermediate Lake should head to the bay in the northeast corner of Siskiwit Lake, a 4-mile paddle from the portage to Malone Bay. In the back is a small cove where the portage marker can clearly be spotted. Those going directly from Wood Lake to Intermediate can weave their way through a string of five small islands that make for a delightful paddle and provide calm conditions, even when a strong northwest wind is blowing.

Siskiwit Lake to Intermediate Lake Portage

Distance: 0.4 mile
Rating: Easy to moderate

This is a relatively level and easy portage through an area frequented by moose. The trail departs Siskiwit Lake and quickly passes a small pond. From here you follow a low ridge, passing more swamps, and then make a gentle descent to Intermediate Lake, reaching the shore in a small inlet at its western end.

INTERMEDIATE LAKE

The portages to Intermediate Lake, the only way to reach that body of water, are almost directly across from each other at the west and east ends. The lake is a mile long and has a depth of 24 feet. Yellow perch can be caught here, but the lake is best known for its population of northern pike, which are often found among the weed beds and small coves in the western half. Like Lake Whittlesey, it's worth stopping here for a night if for no other reason than its somewhat remote location means light fishing pressure.

A cove in the northeast corner of the lake is formed by a peninsula and halfway along its south side is Intermediate Lake Canoe Campground. The facility has three individual sites near the water but the rocky shoreline makes getting in and out of a boat challenging. It cannot be reached from the Lake Richie portage trail.

Intermediate Lake to Lake Richie Portage

Distance: 0.6 mile
Rating: Moderate

The trail begins with a gradual climb from the shoreline of Intermediate Lake and becomes a level walk in the woods until you skirt a noticeable rock bluff. The path rounds the bluff and dips and climbs over the rocky terrain before leveling out. The final portion is a sharp 30-yard drop to the shoreline of Lake Richie.

The trail emerges on the upper arm of Lake Richie. On the other side, at the mouth of the inlet, is the Lake Richie Canoe Campground. The three-site campground is a short paddle away and a scenic spot to spend an evening as much of the lake can be viewed from the rock bluffs that form the shoreline here.

14   The South Shore

❖ *The South Shore* ❖ *Siskiwit Bay*
❖ *The West End* ❖ *Rainbow Cove*
❖ *Grace Harbor* ❖ *Washington Harbor*

Distance: 53 miles (Daisy Farm to Windigo)
Paddling time: 5-7 days
Portages: 1
Longest portage: 0.8 miles

For kayakers who have open-water experience, the right equipment and time, a paddle along the south shore of the Island, from Daisy Farm in Rock Harbor to Washington Harbor, can be an exciting adventure. The trip includes good scenery, solitude, and the Lady herself. There is something to be said for paddling Lake Superior where you have the Island's rocky coastline on one side and the lake's endless surface on the other.

In much of this stretch, kayakers have an advantage because there are no facilities for power boaters, no access trails for hikers, and no protected water for canoeists. It is strongly recommend that canoeists do not attempt the south shore. Lake Superior's sudden squalls and rough seas would quickly swamp an open craft such as a canoe. Though the south shore has more coves and beaches than the north side, emergency landings can still be tricky.

Unless you plan to paddle from Siskiwit Bay to Rainbow Cove in a single day, a paddle that would take 10-14 hours in ideal conditions, you must obtain a special permit from NPS officials to camp in

Kayakers paddle the open water of Lake Superior around Isle Royale.

undesignated areas. This allows you to break the long paddle into 2 or more days, but keep in mind that some areas are closed to cross-country camping, including most offshore islands.

Kayakers should have tight-fitting storm skirts to prevent waves from flooding their boats. Preferably, they should also have plastic foam or other padding under their seat. Lake Superior can be cold, and you'll need more than a couple of layers of fiberglass between your bottom and the water.

Although the paddle from Daisy Farm to Windigo can be done in 3 days, it is best to plan on 5-7, with an extra day scheduled in for rough water. A good itinerary would be to go from Daisy Farm to Chippewa Harbor or Malone Bay the first day and then on to Attwood Beach or Long Point the second day. You could then complete the paddle with a night spent at Rainbow Cove and Feldtmann Lake before paddling into Washington Harbor the third day.

At Washington Harbor only experienced kayakers should continue on around the north shore. Once past Huginnin Cove, the shore consists of steep cliffs and bluffs without adequate places to beach during rough weather. There is little debate that the north shore receives the worst that Lake Superior has to offer.

You can either end your trip at Washington Harbor or hop on *Voyageur II* with your kayak and be transported to McCargoe Cove or the Five Fingers area (see chapter 4).

❖   ❖   ❖   ❖

THE SOUTH SHORE

The 15-mile trip from Daisy Farm Campground to Malone Bay can be undertaken as one long paddle or broken into a pair of easy days with a stop at Chippewa Harbor. The harbor is a beautiful place to spend an evening, and an extra day will allow you to explore the handful of bays and coves along this stretch.

From the dock at Daisy Farm, you cut across Rock Harbor toward the restored Edisen Fishery (see chapter 10) before swinging into Middle Island Passage, which Rock Harbor Lighthouse is so carefully watching. This opening is often choppy, especially with a southerly wind blowing, because the Lake Superior surf is being funneled into Rock Harbor. Caution must be used here, but keep in mind that just south of the lighthouse you can swing into Tonkin Bay for protection.

Continuing along the outside coast there are several small coves and then Conglomerate Bay, a beautiful body of water with a shoreline that is steep in many places and extends almost a mile to the west. At one time the bay was best known for its greenstones and agates found along the water's edge. In another 1.5 miles south, you pass Lea Cove, one of the last bits of protected shoreline on the way to Chippewa Harbor, and then round Saginaw Point which forms its west side.

The shoreline of the Island is now extending west, and for the next 3 miles a protected beach to land at is hard to find. But if conditions are calm, it's a scenic paddle along a rugged coastline until you round a point into the mouth of Chippewa Harbor, marked by a handful of islets and rocks guarding its entrance. The Chippewa Harbor Campground dock is just beyond the narrow passage into the main body of the harbor (see map on page 163).

A rugged shoreline continues west beyond the harbor, offering little protection from the swells of Lake Superior. In the next 2 miles there are few, if any, places to land as you paddle past a rocky coast of bluffs and even an occasional formation that resembles a sea arch. The first and best place to land is Blueberry Cove, so deep and well protected that its surface rarely has a ripple in it, even when there are 3-foot swells on the lake.

Within a mile of Blueberry Cove, you pass Greenstone Beach and Vodrey Harbor, but landing at these shallow coves can still be difficult if a strong wind is blowing out of the south. All worries about open Lake Superior ends when you reach the protective bay formed by Schooner Island, reached 6.5 miles from Chippewa Harbor. You depart the bay through a narrow and shallow gap between the island and the main shoreline and then paddle around a head through the last stretch of open water on the way to Malone Bay.

Lake Superior will be rushing toward a gap formed by Hat Island, and caution must be used here as she pushes you towards the calm water on the other side of the opening. At times the contrast here is remarkable: On one side Lake Superior is hurling herself at the shoreline in whitecaps and waves, while just behind Hat Island there's barely a ripple.

In the final 1.5 miles, you follow the passage formed by the north shores of Hat, Ross, and Malone islands, a scenic paddle that ends when the dock to the Malone Bay Ranger Station comes into view. For kayakers it's better to land on the other side of the wooded point where red-pebbled beaches put you closer to Malone Bay Campground.

❖   ❖   ❖   ❖

SISKIWIT BAY

From Malone Bay Campground the paddling is easy for 2 miles as you head west through well-protected Malone Bay. Keep an eye out for moose on the small islands that border the bay or cut across to Wright Island, where there is an old fish camp at its west end.

Once you pass Wright Island you enter Siskiwit Bay, and the water will probably be noticeably rougher. The large bay is separated from Lake Superior by a thin reef that runs from Point Houghton for more than 7 miles to Menagerie Island. Although the reef breaks up Superior's surf and slow rollers, Siskiwit can still get surprisingly rough, with 3-foot waves and whitecaps possible any time; even 6-footers have been known to form on the bay.

Once past Wright Island and Hopkins Harbor, it's like paddling the open water of Lake Superior for the next 2 miles until after rounding the head formed by Butterfield Point and Spruce Point. The head marks the protection of Hay Bay and from here it should be an easy paddle into this beautiful body of water. The narrow bay is well protected and a good place to hang out if Siskiwit Bay is kicking up.

Hay Bay Campground

Located toward the bottom half of the peninsula that forms Hay Bay, or a 7.5-mile paddle from Malone Bay, Hay Bay Campground is small but pleasant. The site has a dock, a pit toilet, and space for tents. It is also easy to cut across the narrow neck of land to the rocky shore of Siskiwit Bay.

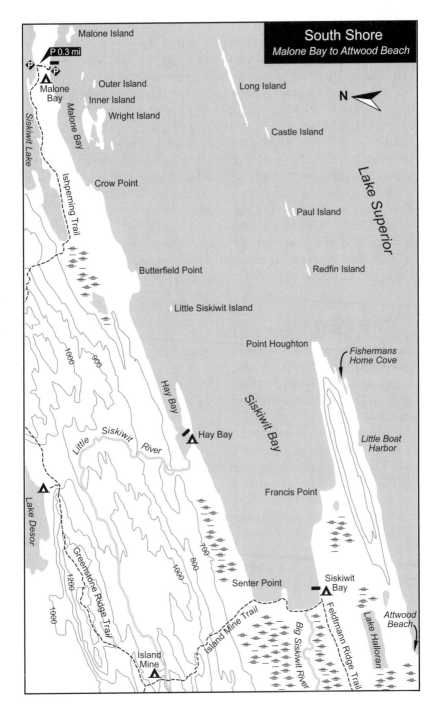

South Shore
Malone Bay to Attwood Beach

Malone Island

P 0.3 mi

Malone Bay

Outer Island

Inner Island

Wright Island

Long Island

Castle Island

N

Lake Superior

Siskiwit Lake

Malone Bay

Ishpeming Trail

Crow Point

Paul Island

Butterfield Point

Redfin Island

Little Siskiwit Island

Point Houghton

Fishermans Home Cove

1000

900

Hay Bay

Siskiwit Bay

Little Boat Harbor

Little Siskiwit River

Hay Bay

Lake Desor

Francis Point

700

Greenstone Ridge Trail

1000

800

Senter Point

Siskiwit Bay

1200

1000

Island Mine Trail

Big Siskiwit River

Feldtmann Ridge Trail

Attwood Beach

Lake Halloran

Island Mine

At the head of the bay is the mouth of Little Siskiwit River, where you can fish for brook and rainbow trout in the river's swift sections and deeper pools. Those with the time and the adventurous spirit can hike up the river to see numerous beaver dams and lodges.

At Hay Point, kayakers have an option of either paddling straight across to Point Houghton or following the shoreline of Siskiwit Bay to reach the same destination. The crossing from Point Hay to Point Houghton, a 3-mile paddle through open water, is a risky venture in rough weather. In good weather, the crossing takes 1.5-2 hours, and at one point you'll find yourself 1.5 miles from the nearest land. With the lake's (and the bay's) ability to kick up suddenly, kayakers have to be prepared in case this should happen.

A safer alternative is to follow the shoreline to the head of Siskiwit Bay, with the possibility of overnighting at Siskiwit Bay Campground, one of the more pleasant areas to pitch a tent. The swing along the shoreline to Point Houghton is a 9 to 10-mile paddle.

❖   ❖   ❖   ❖

THE WEST END

Once you paddle around Point Houghton and pass the day beacon at the tip of the peninsula, you are again in Lake Superior. For most kayakers this moment is accompanied by a tingle down their spine as they stare across the wide expanse of water that is the largest Great Lake.

You quickly pass several small coves, the third being Fisherman's Home Cove, the site of an old fishing camp and a good place to take a break because it offers well-protected water. But remember, all buildings are private and should not be entered.

If the lake is calm, paddling this stretch in the afternoon can be a unique experience. With the sun sinking in the west, its rays will reflect off the water for an intense heat. You are cooled, however, by drops of water from Lake Superior that trickle off your paddle onto your face and arms. If a southerly wind is gently pushing you from behind, the paddling becomes a series of effortless strokes.

The scenery along the South Shore is superb because you pass numerous small coves and inlets composed of red-pebble beaches. There are many spots where you can stop for the night, but the best are Attwood Beach and Long Point.

It's a 10-mile paddle from Fisherman's Home Cove to Long Point. Here you will find long stretches of beach, many open spaces on the

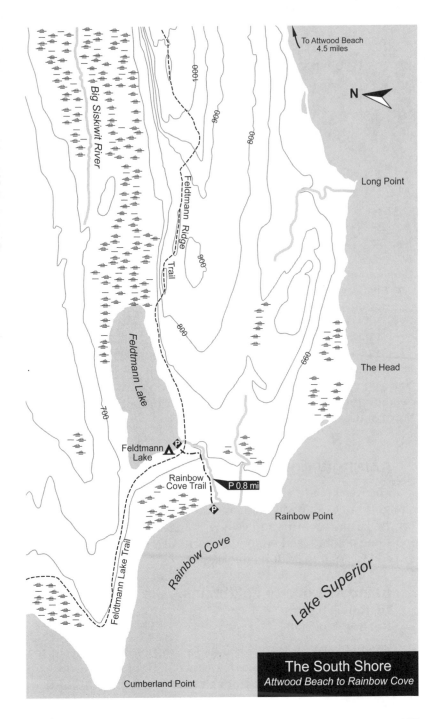

To Attwood Beach
4.5 miles

N

Big Siskiwit River

Feldtmann Ridge Trail

1000

900

800

900

800

700

660

Long Point

The Head

Feldtmann Lake

Feldtmann Lake

Rainbow Cove Trail

P 0.8 mi

Rainbow Point

Feldtmann Lake Trail

Rainbow Cove

Lake Superior

Cumberland Point

The South Shore
Attwood Beach to Rainbow Cove

During a sunset on a clear evening Rainbow Cove is one of the most beautiful places in Isle Royale National Park.

point, and the remains of several buildings. The point was first used as a lumber camp and then was the site of the Saul Fishery.

From Long Point paddle toward The Head, 2 miles away. The Head is marked by a series of caves at the water level, some so large that you can paddle into them during calm weather. It takes a few paddle strokes before you round The Head and spot the tip of Rainbow Point.

❖　　　❖　　　❖　　　❖

RAINBOW COVE

The Head marks a change in direction as you swing north for a straight shot to Rainbow Point and the entrance to the prettiest cove on the Island. Stop for an evening, wander along Rainbow Cove's red-stone beaches, and enjoy the spectacular sunsets. At the southern end is a trail to Feldtmann Lake.

Rainbow Cove to Feldtmann Lake Portage
Distance: 0.8 mile
Rating: Moderate

The trailhead on the cove is 220 yards north of a stream that empties from Feldtmann Lake. The easy trail is surprisingly dry, considering the swamp it passes through. It is level most of the distance

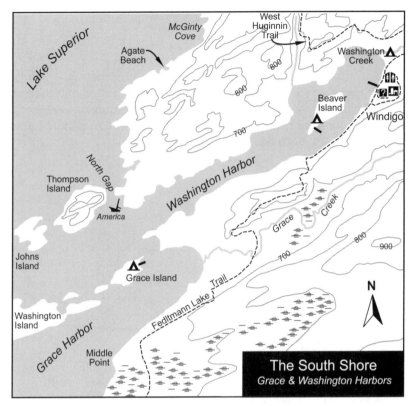

The South Shore
Grace & Washington Harbors

except for a slight rise in the middle, where it swings away from the stream and drops to Feldtmann Lake Campground.

Kayakers should consider portaging their boats into Feldtmann Lake for early-morning fishing. The lake is renowned for its fine pike fishing but rarely sees any action beyond the shore fishermen who hike in. With a kayak, anglers can fish the undisturbed middle or north-shore portions of the lake and have a chance of landing a pike that exceeds 30 or 40 inches.

❖   ❖   ❖   ❖

GRACE HARBOR

From Rainbow Cove you can make a straight shot to Cumberland Point and paddle into the entrance of Grace Harbor, where Washington and Grace islands give paddlers some protection from Lake Superior's large swells. The paddle from Rainbow Cove to Windigo can be accomplished in 3 hours in good weather. Those with an extra day can overnight at Grace Island Campground.

Grace Island Campground

This small campground has two shelters, pit toilets, and a dock. The view is nice from the shelters, and nearby a sand spit extends into the harbor. Almost directly across from the campground on the Island is the mouth of Grace Creek, an ideal place to paddle in the evening to look for moose or fish for trout.

WASHINGTON HARBOR

From Grace Island you paddle north around Card Point and swing east into the mouth of Washington Harbor for Windigo. The 3-mile long harbor is broken up at its east end by Beaver Island.

There are many coves and inlets along the harbor. You can reach them by boat and then fish for brook or rainbow trout. Another interesting paddle in the area is to head west to the mouth of the harbor and then swing north through North Gap, which separates Thompson Island from the rest of Isle Royale. In North Gap, a buoy marks the sunken ship America, the passenger and freight steamer that sank June 7, 1928. One end of the ship lies only a few feet below the surface and can be easily viewed from the seat of a kayak.

Once past Thompson Island, you return to the open waters of Lake Superior along the roughest shoreline of the Island.

Beaver Island Campground

This shoreline campground has three shelters, pit toilets, and a dock but, unfortunately, no individual sites. The campground is a popular one with powerboaters during the summer, and it might be hard to secure a shelter just paddling in. All the shelters face the water, and a short trail leads off to the west end of the island where you can view most of Washington Harbor.

Afterword

The Last Portage

I repositioned the boat on my shoulders and looked up the trail. There were sharp rocks, a steep pitch, and a switchback in front of me. Lord, what a portage! It was what one paddlemate of mine used to call a "grunt": all work, no fun. I climbed higher and with every step the muscles in my thighs burned while my shoulders throbbed under the weight of the yoke.

Going from Duncan Bay to Tobin Harbor is no easy hike. Do it while balancing a canoe over your head and it can be murder – or seem like it. But this was my last portage, and that was by design. I attempt this route only after the food bags have been emptied and the arms strengthened by long days of paddling through the Island.

If the red path to Lake Richie is the first portage for many of us, this climb over the Greenstone Ridge is the last. On one you enter the wilderness of Isle Royale, on the other you leave it. You struggle up the side of the ridge only to break out of the trees on the crest of the Greenstone with a sudden realization: The trip is over. It's a moment of vivid contrasts. You're standing on the Island's longest foot trail while holding a boat, on the edge between the quiet backcountry of Duncan Bay and the roar of a seaplane taking off in Tobin Harbor.

It's also a moment of indecisiveness. There is an urge to hurry south to Rock Harbor, to soft beds, warm showers, and food that can be consumed without a cup of boiling water and a 10-minute wait.

The spoils after a long trek. Backpackers dropped their packs before heading into the Rock Harbor Snack Bar.

But then you turn and look north toward Duncan Harbor, where the day before a bull emerged along its shoreline and tipped its rack to you or a pike grabbed that lure and ran so hard it broke your line.

You think about the loons that laugh at night and the portages you endured every day. There were the quiet moments spent watching the sun melt into Lake Superior and the celebration for catching a Lake Whittlesey walleye and the fresh feast that followed in the middle of nowhere. Then you realize it's not the moose or walleye or even incredible scenery that appealed to you but the simplicity of the Island's backcountry. To travel without a motor, to stuff everything you need into a pack, to leave the cell phone at home, this is what nourishes you on Isle Royale. This is why you came.

And standing on the crest of the Greenstone Ridge, I suddenly had this desire to retreat north from where I had just come, to stay in the backcountry, to spend another day in a place where the only deadline I had was to pitch the tent before dark.

But we can't. The circle must be completed. If you hike in, eventually you have to climb back out. The backcountry is a temporary experience, for in this wilderness only the moose and wolves can stay. You and I have to return to the city, taking home only memories and the knowledge that what lies between the red path and the last portage is worth every grunt.

More Information

The Isle Royale & Keweenaw Parks Association (IRKPA) is a nonprofit organization that publishes and sells a variety of books and pamphlets about the park. Many cover the colorful history of the Island, and  others look into the special wolf-moose relationship. There are also many field guides that help backpackers understand and enjoy the wilderness they travel through.

The following are a few of the books that might interest hikers and canoeists:

Borealis: An Isle Royale Potpourri edited by David Harmon. The stories of people who shaped the history of Isle Royale.

Elfin World of Mosses and Liverworts of Michigan's Upper Peninsula and Isle Royale by Janice Glime. A field guide to the mosses and liverworts of Isle Royale and beyond.

Fishes of Isle Royale by K. F. Lagler and C. R. Goldman. General guide to sport fishing for the park.

Flora of Isle Royale by A. Slavick and R. Janke. A catalog of all the vascular plants found on the Island.

Isle Royale: A Photographic History by Thomas and Kendra Gale. The history of Isle Royale in narrative, historical photographs and maps.

Island Life: An Isle Royale Nature Guide by Ted Gostomski and Janet Marr. A guide to the the common flora and fauna of Isle Royale, covering more than 350 species of mammals, birds, reptiles, trees and flowers. Easy to use and easy to pack along on the trail.

Superior Wilderness: Isle Royale National Park by Napier Shelton. Complete natural history of the park, with color illustrations and animal checklists.

The Wildflowers of Isle Royale by R. A. and N. Janke. Drawings and descriptions of common wildflowers found on the Island.

The books are on sale at Rock Harbor and Windigo visitor centers, and at the park headquarters at Houghton. You can also order them ahead of time or receive a complete publication list by contacting the IRKPA at (800) 678-6925 or online through its web site at *www.irkpa.org.*

Index

The Author

Jim DuFresne has a deep rooted passion for two things; sunsets and shorelines, no doubt the result of living his entire life in the two states that have more coastline than any other; Alaska and Michigan.

Within a year of graduating from Michigan State University with a journalism degree, Jim moved to Juneau, Alaska as the outdoors and sports editor of the *Juneau Empire* and became the first Alaskan sportswriter to win a national award from the Associated Press. More signifi-cant than the writing award, he dis-

Jim DuFresne

covered his passion for the mountains and wilderness travel while living in Alaska's capital city.

In 1981, Jim spent a winter in New Zealand to backpack and write his first book, *Tramping in New Zealand* for Lonely Planet. He followed up with the first edition of Lonely Planet's *Alaska* and later *Hiking in Alaska* and then returned to Michigan to write *Isle Royale National Park: Foot Trails & Water Routes*. The guide to the wilderness areas of Isle Royale has been in publication in various editions for almost 30 years and today is known as the "backpacker's bible" to the Lake Superior island.

Today Jim lives in Michigan where he's never more than an hour's drive from the shoreline of a Great Lake. He is the main con-tributor to ***www.MichiganTrailMaps.com***, a resource web site de-voted to trail users and the promotion of trails in his home state. Among his other tiles are *Backpacking In Michigan* and *12 Classic Trout Streams in Michigan: A Handbook for Fly Anglers* (University of Michigan Press), *Michigan: Off the Beaten Path* (Globe Pequot Publica-tions), *50 Hikes In Michigan* (Backcountry Publications) and *Porcupine Mountains Wilderness State Park* (Thunder Bay Press).